THE $100 BILLION ALLOWANCE

Accessing the Global Teen Market

ELISSA MOSES

John Wiley & Sons, Inc.

New York • Chichester • Weinheim • Brisbane • Singapore • Toronto

Photographs in Chapter 5 are by Ian Tong.

For Emmy and Zack, the two best teenagers.

Contents

Acknowledgments

Creating this book was an exciting journey of discovery and collaboration.

First, I want to thank the people who helped the book spring to life—Allyn Freeman, Kirsten Miller, Kathy Baldwin, Ian Tong, M. R. Carey, and my wise editors, Ruth Mills, Airié Dekidjiev, and Linda Witzling.

A very special thanks to Chip Walker, who was my partner and traveling companion in much of the research described in this book, and whose insights are invaluable in understanding global teen culture.

The research on which this book is based was made possible by two forward-thinking CEOs—Roy Bostock, chairman of the MacManus Group, who believed in the value of the New World Teen Study to D'Arcy Masius Benton & Bowles and its clients; and Cor Boonstra, president of Royal Philips Electronics N.V., who is visionary in his understanding of the importance of the global consumer in building leadership brands.

I have been lucky in my career to have mentors to inspire and guide my work—most directly Dr. Joseph Plummer, who captured my dreams with his lifestyle segmentation work in the 1970s, and who made the dreams a reality when he was my coach on the New World Teen Study 20 years later. Thanks to Hans Lopater, Marvin Belkin, and the late Ray Berland and Dr. Ken Warwick for teaching me the unwavering standards of reliable research and segmentation techniques. Also thanks to two of the great marketing inspirers who have crossed my path—Gerard Dufour and Sergio Zyman. I have learned much from their genius.

I also want to acknowledge some of the people who helped invaluably along the way—Gia Medieiros, Mariette Papic, Alex Zion, Patricia Fessler, Natalya Vinokurova, Hilarine Francis, and trends visionary Marian Salzman; also Gabe Fisch of Essex Tabulating. Also, a special thanks to Laurie Meadoff, founder of the CityKids Foundation, who helped me get to know and understand some of the best representatives of this new generation.

Much of what I know about teens I learned from my clients while I was managing director at the BrainWaves Group, especially Randy Ransom, John Duke, Noel Marts, and Claire Quinn at The Coca-Cola Company; Roy Edmonson and Judy Jones at Levi's; Janet Scardino at MTV; Peter Gumas and David Land at the NBA; and Jan Murley at Procter & Gamble.

Thanks to Pamela Rogers, qualitative research expert par excellence, who has long been a powerful sounding board and treasured friend.

I want to thank my father, Dr. Harry Moses, for teaching me as a scientist to "never assume anything"; my mother, Edith Moses, for showing me how to talk to just about anybody about anything; and my on-call advisors, brothers Bruce and Alan Moses.

Finally, I want to thank my wonderful husband Mark Shornick and teenagers Emily and Zachary, who were incredibly supportive and generous in allowing me the time (and quiet) to complete this book. Note to family: It's okay to turn the volume back up on the CD players and TVs now.

A Special Note of Thanks

The New World Teen Study, which serves as the foundation for this book, was made possible by the funding, support, and vision of D'Arcy Masius Benton & Bowles. I would like to express my thanks and gratitude to D'Arcy for making this understanding of global teen culture possible.

D'Arcy is a worldwide leader among advertising agencies dedicated to understanding consumer needs and wants. When the message became clear that greater insight was needed to help international clients such as Coca-Cola, Procter & Gamble, Philips, and Burger King market empathetically to youth, a major commitment was made to conduct substantive research. The New World Teen Study is the most comprehensive research study to understand youth attitudes, values, and behavior ever undertaken. It required a significant investment of time for senior professional staff and out-of-pocket expenditures. Without the vision and special support of Roy Bostock, Arthur Selkowitz, Craig Brown, Chip Walker, Hank Bernstein, and Joe Plummer, none of this learning would have been possible.

Part of the magic of the New World Teen Study was the agencywide teamwork and cooperation it inspired. Many, many people who participated throughout the D'Arcy global network deserve my thanks.

1

Welcome to Teen Planet: Population 560 Million

A group of 10 to 12 teenagers sits huddled against the wall of an underpass in Prague to escape the rain. It is Saturday afternoon. Despite living in a developing country, these teens are not unlike their age counterparts around the globe. Like all youth everywhere, they enjoy hanging out together, exchanging private jokes, blasting music on a boom box, and flirting. What makes this group different from the last generation of teens in Prague? They have hope—hope for personal freedom, hope for a secure, stable lifestyle, and hope for economic opportunity. Ten years ago, the same statement could not be made.

We all live in hopeful times. The times are hopeful for the half-billion new world teens ages 15 to 19 who span the globe, and they are hopeful for marketers with dreams of expanding their market shares and building relationships with this new generation. Most teens have a significant amount of money to spend. In fact, teens spend more than $100 billion every year. Heavy spending is not

1

just indigenous to the United States. In fact, if we examine where teens spend the most on a weekly basis, 4 of the 6 inhabited continents are represented in the list of the top 10 countries.

Top 10 Countries: Average Weekly Teen Spending	
1. Norway	$49.70
2. Sweden	$41.70
3. Brazil	$41.30
4. Argentina	$40.50
5. Hong Kong	$38.00
6. United States	$37.60
7. Denmark	$37.40
8. Singapore	$34.10
9. Greece	$32.90
10. France	$31.30

Teens inhabit every country on every continent. From Manhattan to Madras and Milan to Melbourne, teens who speak different languages (although many speak English) all speak the same dialect of global brand consumption. In many of the huge developing nations, such as China, India, and Brazil, youth under 25 dominate the population.

Marketers at the doorstep of the new millennium face a dynamic opportunity to grow by offering products and services to a global youth culture. In some sense, there is a gold rush going on. The world is getting more affluent and access to consumer goods is ubiquitous. As if overnight, a new crop of young consumers who want everything has emerged.

The kids in Prague are especially similar to the teens in East Germany, Russia, Brazil, Peru, China, and all the other developing countries that were never a practical consideration in building a global youth target market in the past. The significant difference is that a global youth culture has now emerged that marketers can access with cost-efficient means.

In this book I help marketers navigate the secret routes to reach global youth, pointing out the bumps in the road and helping marketers prepare to handle the detours as they arise. What I know with certainty is that we are at the starting gate of the biggest teen sales and marketing opportunity in world history. Marketers who take advantage of this global culture shift will create brand equity that will pay off for years to come.

What youth marketers need most is a true understanding of global youth culture and a framework for developing marketing programs. In this book I systematically provide information on the following factors:

Market sizing.   The size of the teen population and what they spend.

Cultural unifiers.   The elements that serve as the foundation for global youth culture and provide the shortcuts for achieving efficient economies of scale in marketing programs.

Cultural differentiators.   The key differences that keep global teens from being homogenous and that marketers need to take into consideration to avoid being perceived as aggressive or irrelevant.

Values segmentation.   The underlying value structure that defines teens by their innermost values and priorities in life. The values segmentation enables marketers to understand the motivational dynamic of teens country by country and define targets based on like minds rather than geography.

Regional/key country perspective.   A view of the world on a national and regional basis that puts geography into perspective.

Case histories.   Examples of leading global youth marketers I know firsthand who have put the framework to work to their advantage.

Equipped with this perspective, youth marketers can enable themselves to develop brand strategies that have a far better chance of succeeding in the global marketplace. They will also have the advantage of saving valuable time and substantial investment in market research. The job has already been done for them.

The Here and Now

Up until today, global marketing was an overwhelming undertaking. The world was culturally diverse, markets were fractionated, and the cost of research and marketing was prohibitive.

But something changed. For global youth, culture became one. One unified and cohesive group emerged, which I call the *new world teens*.

One of the most important events to global teens was that MTV pioneered a network available to 287 million homes across 88 countries, making information accessible to teens throughout the world. MTV became the global youth equivalent of Radio Free Europe.

How do I know all these facts? Well, I have immersed myself in global teen culture for the past five years. As founder and managing director of The BrainWaves Group (a global research and trends consulting firm), and now as senior vice president and director of global intelligence for Royal Philips Electronics N.V., I have traveled the world conducting surveys, talking to teens, and observing young consumers in their natural habitats.

As a strategic marketing consultant to The Coca-Cola Company, Levi's, the National Basketball Association (NBA), MTV, Nike, Philips, Burger King, Kodak, Calvin Klein, and others, I have grappled with introducing global icons to a new teen generation. I have seen marketers let opportunities slip through their channels of distribution. I have witnessed firsthand costly mistakes, especially in regard to global teens.

But more times than not, I have participated in making marketing magic—pouring new life into old brands to reach a fresh generation. I get excited introducing new products. I have experienced the thrill of watching this young global cohort adopt new brands to which it will be forever connected.

Why have I concentrated on this youth segment? Because I love teenagers. I love them because they think independently, because they are full of creativity, and because they are buoyantly optimistic about the world.

Teens like to laugh, love to have fun, and are wise beyond their years. They refuse to be bamboozled. They won't take no for an answer. And, as a marketer, I love global teens because they are unabashed consumers without losing their human values.

It all started because as director of strategic planning at D'Arcy Masius Benton & Bowles Advertising in New York, a lot of my clients had brands with a teen focus: Clearasil, Burger King, Coca-Cola, and Umbro, among others. The creators of the Disney Institute even consulted me on how to position an attraction to families with kids older than 12.

Over time, in meeting after meeting, I heard the same assumptions about teens from boomer-aged creative directors, account supervisors, and product managers. We all came of age during the volatile 1960s and 1970s, when anyone over 30 was not to be trusted. We assumed that teens today behaved the same and shared the same attitudes as our hippie generation: Teens were rebellious, cynical, and prone to escapism.

Soon afterward, my research and travel schedule began fast and furiously. Much to my amazement, I felt that I was sitting on the edge of a breakthrough discovery. The surprise: Today's youth were completely different from all our preconceived hypotheses.

An alarm went off in my head: If our clients did not change the tone and content of their teen communication, they would fail to attract this segment as consumers.

I told my management at D'Arcy that what I had discovered was the tip of the teen fact-finding iceberg. The agency offered financial support, and I embarked on the research journey of a lifetime.

The New World Teen Study would ultimately be a two-phase quantitative survey of 34,000 teens throughout 44 countries (6,400 teens in Wave I, and 27,600 in Wave II). In addition, I would talk one-on-one and in focus groups to teens all over the globe. It became the single largest research undertaking for understanding global youth values, lifestyles, and consumer behavior ever conducted. The teen study changed forever the way our clients thought about youth marketing. And as an added plus, this knowledge opened the doors to many new clients.

The big payoff was that several clients achieved success with many new and revised international marketing programs by using the study.

Now it's time to share this learning with you.

Let's start with the most significant fact. There are 560 million teens between the ages of 15 and 19 worldwide. And most have money to spend. Their spending totals more than $100 billion a year in urban and suburban cities throughout the world.

As I said, teens inhabit every country on every continent. Their greatest numbers are in China, India, Brazil, Indonesia, and the United States. Teens who speak different languages all speak the same language of global brand consumption.

What I've discovered, having logged more than 1 million miles of worldwide air travel and having interviewed many thousands of teens, is that a unified youth culture has emerged. For the first time in history, national barriers are down.

Theodore Levitt wrote almost 20 years ago that "a powerful force now drives the world towards a single converging commonality and that force is technology." Levitt was right, just ahead of his time, because technology is today's teen's ticket to the future.

There's more good news: This entire teen generation perceives much of the world in the same way. You can thank the global expansion of television, including MTV and CNN, communication via the Internet, and the accessibility of hundreds of the same global consumer brands. Teens have become one culture because of shared cultural experience.

Shown here are some of the activities global youth participate in at majority levels. These types of common experiences are an essential part of creating a unified culture.

Global Teen Media Habits

- 85 percent watch MTV or music videos.
- 81 percent use computers.
- 81 percent enjoy movie comedies.
- 73 percent watch the Olympics.
- 71 percent enjoy watching or playing basketball.

Plugged In, Well Connected

Global teen consumers have their antennae up and are hungry for the hottest information through any and all sources. This is what makes building a global teen brand both possible and cost efficient. If a marketer makes a noise in Cincinnati, it can be heard by teens throughout the world. Unlike previous generations that wanted to "tune in, turn on, drop out," today's global teens do not want to miss out on anything. The world is just too exciting, and the free flow of information from television, computers, radio, and even cellular phones is too irresistible to ignore.

Just glance at these statistics on how teens worldwide give and receive information:

- 85 percent have telephones.
- 81 percent use computers.
- 79 percent watch television daily.
- 73 percent listen to the radio at least weekly.
- 69 percent read magazines monthly.
- 68 percent read newspapers weekly.
- 43 percent watch the news often.

The truly remarkable fact is that so many of these sources are frequently accessed all at the same time. This, I'm convinced, is because today's teen is an advancement of the species, having evolved capabilities for multitasking that are far beyond the comprehension of previous age groups. In fact, if you want to make teens really nervous, place them in a quiet room without access to any of these information sources.

The Love of Brand Names

Why are brand names so important to teens? Because in an age of information overload, teens want assurance that they are making the right judgments that will enhance their identity. A brand says a lot about who they are and where they stand in life.

While on a business trip to China last year, a colleague visited a 16-year-old boy in his family's small apartment in Shanghai. Inside was a Philips television set with the tags left on. The proud family wanted to demonstrate its ability to purchase famous name brands and state-of-the-art technology. It was also proud that it could give technological benefits to the son, with a new computer still in the box. But space was limited, and there was no place yet to set the computer up.

In Brazil, I strolled through an American-style shopping mall in São Paulo on a Saturday afternoon as groups of teenagers lingered at a promotional kiosk. What product attracted these kids like bees to honey? It was Fruit of the Loom underwear. A commodity product in the United States, but a celebrated, and cool, American import in Brazil. More than just a brand name, it represented an important status symbol for Brazilian teens.

America Is Where the Action Is

One of the biggest shocks of the multinational teen research was how cool America is outside of the United States. This is a far cry from the early 1970s, when I traveled through Europe as a teen myself amid some latent "ugly American" sentiment. In those days, lots of the U.S. kids pretended to be Canadian to avoid nasty comments and confrontations.

Now, fast-forward 30 years to the year 2000. Almost every teen you meet speaks English with an American accent from having watched hours of American television. These kids are wearing American clothes, watching American movies, playing American video games, using American software, eating American food, drinking American soft drinks, and—above all—dreaming the American dreams. In fact, the United States is cited more than any other country as the nation with the greatest influence on teen fashion and culture.

Country Teens Cite as Having the Greatest Influence on Fashion and Culture*

Country	Percentage
America	68
France	26
England	14
Japan	10
Italy	8
China	4
Europe (nonspecific)	4
India	4
Germany	3
Hong Kong	3

*Multiple answers accepted.

What exactly is the American Dream for youth? Today it has become synonymous with the Chinese Dream, the Brazilian Dream, even the French Dream. The universal dream is to lead a good life with a rewarding job, have satisfying family relationships, enjoy rich experiences, manifest freedom and self-expression, and possess lots of consumer goods.

The United States has exported the American Dream—translated loosely as the freedom to consume—and youth the world over have accepted it completely.

Teens throughout the world who become interested in a brand today have a much greater chance of having a relationship with it through adulthood. The important fact is that if you can reach these kids early, it will translate into lifetime value and create efficiencies of spending in marketing dollars. It is more efficient to retain a satisfied user than to pay expensive start-up costs to convert users of competing products.

Global Brands Score Goals

In Wave II of the New World Teen Study, we showed 27,600 teens logos of international products to gauge their brand awareness and usage. Which are the global giants most recognized by teens? The first five are: (1) Coca-Cola, (2) Sony, (3) Adidas, and (4) tie between Nike and Pepsi. The next tier features: (5) Kodak; (6) Colgate; (7) Fanta; (8) tie between Disney, M&M's, and Reebok; (9) tie between Philips and McDonald's; and (10) tie between Apple, Johnson & Johnson, and the Chicago Bulls.

Surprised? Michael Jordan's superstar status elevated the Bulls, in tenth place, higher than the NBA, which came in thirteenth. Did you know that Kodak and Colgate dominate global teen consciousness? What about Philips, an international leading brand in electronics that is only starting to make inroads into the U.S. teen market? These icons have generated the power to transcend geography and generations.

Brand Relationships

Teens love brands. Brands delight. Brands provide a badge of identity. Brands are enablers. Brands are passports to global culture.

Top 20 brands recognized by teens worldwide (75 brand logos were tested).

1. Coca-Cola

2. SONY

3. adidas

4. NIKE   PEPSI

5. Kodak

6. Colgate

7. fanta

8. Disney   m&m's

   Reebok

9. PHILIPS

   McDonald's

10. Apple Computer   CHICAGO BULLS   Johnson&Johnson

11. IBM   Gillette

12. Enjoy Sprite   Lee   Levi's

13. NBA   VISA

14. FUJI

15. MTV MUSIC TELEVISION

16. Pizza Hut

17. Nintendo

18. CNN

19. SEGA

20. MasterCard

Brands are tickets to success. Brands embody all the good values that life has to offer: fun, attractiveness, and opportunity for a better life.

It's crucial for marketers to understand the relationship between known brands and global youth. This generation has been brought up to regard brands as icons. The brand represents a fortifying assurance of stability that is both solid and ongoing.

Somewhere in the world today a teen scored badly on an algebra test, couldn't locate Kuala Lumpur on a map, had a fight with a sibling, was punished by a parent, discovered that an unrequited love likes another, couldn't stop the winning soccer goal, or broke a bicycle chain.

This teen is feeling down in the dumps. It's more than just a bad hair day. On the way home from school, this teen may buy a Coca-Cola, a Mars candy bar, or a Burger King Whopper. The brands provide solace because they bring *reliable* pleasure.

In a teen world where adults sometimes can't be trusted, brands are familiar and dependable. They promise to deliver the benefits advertised. Teens seek out and trust these products, whose images they have seen all their lives.

Not all brands that succeed with teens are sexy or hip. A good example worldwide is Johnson's shampoo. Teens globally have remained favorable toward this respectable Johnson & Johnson brand, and their affection for it has been unwavering. It's partly an imprinting phenomenon, because Johnson's was probably their first shampoo.

Brands are powerful symbols that advertise and demonstrate how you and your family are doing economically. In the United States we take brands for granted, because a typical supermarket is filled with more than 28,000 different products. Most of these are easy to obtain and not costly. But in countries in Asia and Latin America, brands are a scorecard that indicates how teens are stacking up to their peers.

Why America Is Cool

Youth wants to own the brand that is hottest, the most cool, and of the moment, right now. It is part of the youthful pack mentality. This desire leads to the yearning for products from the United States, because the zenith of teen aspiration is to be as much like American teens as possible. When kids in Germany or Brazil wear Levi's or clothes from The Gap, they participate in that distinctly American experience.

How did America get to be so cool?

I believe the first answer is television. First with sitcoms, dramas, and cartoons, and now with the proliferation of CNN's 24-hour cable news programming, MTV, and other U.S.-originated programming around the globe, television has carried indirect advertising for American lifestyles as well as products. Teens who want to learn English watch these shows regularly and see firsthand the fabric of life available to American teens. When these advertised brands appear locally, teens become motivated to try the latest from American brands.

American sports are also important worldwide in enhancing the image of American cool. It should come as no surprise that the NBA finals dominate the ratings, with a potential global audience of 252 million viewers. Finally, Hollywood movies also reinforce the image of the American teen "good life." Many savvy marketers who think globally realize that these visual depictions of American life subtly sustain the idea that America is a trendy place for teenagers. In one sense, movies and television are the forerunners of the global spread of what is happening in American culture, transporting brand images and often arriving in foreign households before the American brands arrive. Potential implication: Do not underestimate brand placement in television shows and movies.

Teen Influence on Global Parents

Throughout the world, teens act as brand advocates in the household. Many participate in household shopping. But it is the big-ticket items where teens really have an active say.

Parents ask, "Where should we go on vacation this year? What kind of car should we get? Come with us, we're going to buy a new television. What kind of computer do we need? Want to test drive some cars with us?"

As parents universally try to provide a good life for their children, they recognize that kids are often more knowledgeable than they are about products. It is a mark of the times, particularly in the area of technology, that children are the primary consultants when it comes to computers, digital television, cellular phones, and Internet providers.

While we have solid estimates on what teens actually spend directly on an annual basis, it only boggles the imagination to think of how many billions of dollars they control *indirectly*.

The Size of Global Youth

Teens cannot be ignored. One out of four people in the world is between the ages of 10 and 24. One out of every six persons worldwide is between 15 and 19.

Current population statistics reveal that the populations of Latin America, China, India, and other less-developed regions are dramatically skewing younger. In Brazil, for example, 50 percent of the population is under age 25. A glance at the top 10 countries with teens ages 15 to 19 demonstrates this fact. This means that if you are marketing almost any brand to these developing countries, you need to consider youth.

The numbers of teens ages 15 to 19 in China and India alone are staggering. Each country represents more than 90 million teens. To put this in perspective, that is about 9 or 10 times the size of several European countries, such as Austria or Hungary. *No other country comes close to these figures.* Ergo, being the leading teen brand in China or India could conceivably be more lucrative than leading in most other countries combined.

Global teens are fast-food purchasers, clothing buyers, television viewers, telephone users, e-commerce customers, and whatever. They represent enormous numbers for marketers of all goods and services.

The question to be answered in this book is why and how you can reach them in a meaningful way.

Top 10 Countries Where Teens Live— a Regional Analysis

	Population of 15- to 19-year-olds, millions
1. India	101.3
2. China	97.7
3. Indonesia	22.3
4. United States	19.7
5. Brazil	17.8
6. Russia	11.7
7. Mexico	10.7
8. Vietnam	8.5
9. Philippines	8.4
10. Japan	7.7

Source: U.S. Bureau of the Census, International Data Base, 1999.

A Direct Line to Global Youth

The quickest route to millions of global teens is via the entertainment and technology highway and the media and entertainment caravan. Media resources currently in place (and expanding exponentially) can target a message to a single country or to the world virtually overnight.

Currently, marketers can target global youth in the same way as national youth—via television and the computer. Because the message is primarily electronic, advertising or promotion can be generated in New York, London, or Paris.

Two large conveyer belts of global information are MTV and CNN. These provide almost 24 hours per day of music and news that the world can see immediately or tape for later viewing. Thus, if a new Madonna or Ricky Martin video airs on MTV, it is the topic of teen discussion the next day globally.

You cannot underestimate the value of these global communications for reaching a mass target so quickly and effectively. Without mass communications, there would not be the culture or marketing phenomenon of New World Teens.

Ici, On Parle Anglais

A point to emphasize is the adoption of English as the world's second language. Even in the European Union, the language spoken among the members is English.

It's a practical reality. Without knowledge of English, the Internet is not easily navigable. More and more business and other operations will be written primarily in English.

So, teens the world over are jabbering away in U.S. English.

A plus to marketers is that as the world adopts a single language for secondary communication, it becomes easier and more cost-efficient to communicate about products. In some cases it will be possible to create advertising in English that can be aired worldwide without dubbing into local languages and be wholly effective against a given target.

Dual Cultural Passports

Every teen holds two cultural passports: One is for entry into the global market and the other is for entry into the local culture. When multinational companies implement marketing plans to reach global teens, they must decide which of the two routes to travel or, on some occasions, plan to use both.

Using a two-level bridge analogy, the upper level is the global route, the fast lane where marketing events occur globally at a breakneck speed. For example, this is the MTV advertising lane, which allows marketers to reach millions of teens instantaneously overnight. If marketers can identify a globally meaningful commercialization theme for a brand, the savings can be enormous.

The lower level is the local lane. It often proceeds at a more modest rate. It can have bulls-eye relevance and heightened emotional value, but is slowed down by the investment in understanding culture and tradition as well as in setting up local projects. It can mean setting up street basketball hoops in poor neighborhoods in the Philippines or, like McDonald's, sponsoring the U.S. All-American High School Basketball Team. These experiences can be powerful for the participants and can create positive brand relationships that are unwavering. However, there is a higher price to be paid in identifying, executing, and managing local opportunities throughout the world.

Think of the booklets sold at high school football games that are filled with ads for local and national sponsors. This represents a personal commitment at the grassroots level but is much more costly to achieve.

Why? Consider researching every local market if you are marketing a global brand. It takes huge resource investment, lengthy timetables, and backbreaking travel for your executives and consultants. Moreover, it requires individual production costs for commercials, cost of management of local programs, and cost of local buys.

Compare this with a golden-bullet approach—one macro campaign, produced with economies of scale, regional buys, and a multinational agency to handle management. But, macro is better only *if.* The big *if* is getting a central message that has universal relevance and poignancy for a brand. Remember: In the fast lane, teens travel as one.

The best of my clients leverage the new world teen unifiers that are detailed in Chapter 3 and keep an eye on the differentiators explained in Chapter 4. This means understanding the key unifiers and differentiators of teen culture around the world, aiming high to have a single strategy, and then adjusting or supplementing on an as-needed local basis.

The Immutable Life Stage of Teens

One unwavering similarity of what it means to be a global teen is the universality of the maturation process—change, uncertainty, and hormones. These are immutable truths about what it means to be young and a teenager for *every* generation.

A teen's world is sometimes extreme, marked by intense highs and crashing lows. When teens are excited, they can seem out of control. The one thing all teenagers share equally is this state of uncertainty. *Will I get into college? Will I get a good job? Will I get married? Will I be successful? Will I be happy?* Sometimes the future seems rosy, and sometimes overwhelmingly bleak.

So many "first" times happen as a teenager—first love, first accomplishment, and first job. It also marks the time when teens first have their own money to spend. The spending choices are not parental but their own. Teens become full-fledged consumers and not just users.

It is also during this teen period when youths begin to make some crucial purchasing decisions for the first time. They become more brand conscious and brand aware. They define themselves in part by these brands.

Like strange birds in the zoo, a teen's attire can say, "Look at me. This is who I am." In the United States, think of the impact of Tommy Hilfiger on a nation of teens, all proud to show off the red, white, and blue colors. Or the Timberland boot craze. The teen years are a time of self-investigation and the formation of identity as well as style.

Twenty years ago, China was a nation wearing monolithic gray Mao jackets. Today, most Chinese are brightly dressed in western garb. It's as though China transformed itself from black and white to Technicolor overnight. Girls are wearing makeup. It's just another example of changes in Asia that have had an impact on teenagers. Asian teens will continue to dress in western-style clothes or follow new trends that emerge in their own region without any memory of the drab past.

Because of this teen life stage, a time of great uncertainty when all things are both possible and frightening, marketers must employ a radically different psychology to sell and market to this group. They can make a connection by supporting positive solutions and shaping dreams for an uncertain future. And if they are responsible, they should avoid negativity and exploitation of insecurities.

There is a paradox we must all remember. Teens take themselves very seriously while having lots of fun. Marketers can build an honest relationship with teens by addressing their hopes and dreams and understanding the essence of what it always means to be young.

Major Misconceptions about Global Youth

Multinational companies operate today with notable misconceptions about global youth. Some of the false assumptions are the size of the population segment, the amount of money teens spend annually, and how uniform this group is in terms of a shared value structure.

What's vitally important for marketers to understand is that if they understand the common unifiers outlined in Chapter 3, they can reach teens with a similar message that emphasizes the positive similarities among all teens. Since hopes and dreams among teens are fairly universal, an advertising message that reinforces how positive it is to be a teen (and how meaningful) will be acceptable worldwide.

But first, let's examine how big the potential prize is for marketers. The answer lies in how much teens spend in each country and the size of each country's teen population. I call it the *money trail*.

2

The Money Trail

Why did I call this book *The $100 Billion Allowance?* Because I have unique research that reveals how much teens estimate they spend in an average week in 37 countries. When this spending amount is factored by the teen population in each country, the proportion of teens that are middle to upper class, and the number of teens that live in urban or suburban populations, the annual teen spending figure works out to be $119,786,180,178.92 in U.S. dollars—or approximately $100 billion if you care to safely round down.

Of course, we collected the data in local currency and then had to calculate U.S. equivalents on current exchange rates. Even though they may be approximate, the findings are invaluable because they help marketers identify the most fertile markets for their teen-targeted services and waves.

Some countries, such as Denmark, have relatively high weekly spending patterns (average: $37 per week), but the teen population is low (286,000). China, on the other hand, has low weekly spending (average: $5.50) with an enormous teen population (97.7 million). Hence, there are choices to be made.

The first table shows average weekly spending estimates, converted to U.S. dollars among middle-class to upper-middle-class teens surveyed in urban and suburban markets throughout each country.

Perhaps there will be some surprise to see that weekly teen spending is higher in two South American countries—Brazil and Argentina—than it is in the United States. This is due in part to the relative price of foreign goods, such as Nikes and Levi's, as well as runaway inflation that suffers from exchange rates. Nonetheless, there are strong strata of wealth in those less-developed countries, as evidenced by their beautiful shopping centers and elegantly

National Teen Spending per Average Week

Country	$U.S.	Country	$U.S.
Norway	50	Thailand	20
Sweden	42	South Korea	20
Brazil	41	Canada	20
Argentina	40	South Africa	19
Hong Kong	38	Peru	18
United States	38	Spain	16
Denmark	37	Philippines	14
Singapore	34	Mexico	13
Greece	33	Venezuela	12
France	31	Poland	11
Germany	30	Indonesia	9
India	28	Lithuania	9
United Kingdom	26	Russia	7
Australia	25	Nigeria	6
Japan	24	Chile	6
Netherlands	23	Hungary	6
Taiwan	22	China	5
Colombia	22	Vietnam	4
Belgium	21		

dressed upscale populace. Most people who have never set foot in these countries have no idea how sophisticated and refined their local monied classes can be.

Another possible surprise is the high weekly teen spending in the Scandinavian countries—Norway, Sweden, and Denmark. In this case, the numbers reflect strong consumer-oriented economies. Perhaps less obvious is the fact that these 3 countries are in the top-10 list of countries where teens have working mothers. Most likely this contributes to the flow of money into the hands of teens. Moreover, it also corresponds with the countries being in the top-10 list of countries where teens work for money. Teenagers' allowance money, you may remember, is not a discriminating factor in and of itself, because almost every teen gets an allowance. The critical factors are how much allowance money, where else teens get money, and whether teens earn money themselves.

Top 10 Countries: Weekly Teen Spending, Teens Working for Money, and Teens with Working Mothers

Rank	Weekly Spending	Work for Money	Mother Works
1	Norway	Denmark	China
2	Sweden	United States	Denmark
3	Brazil	Australia	Finland
4	Argentina	Netherlands	Hungary
5	Hong Kong	Norway	Vietnam
6	United States	United Kingdom	Sweden
7	Denmark	Israel	Estonia
8	Singapore	Canada	Norway
9	Greece	Sweden	Lithuania
10	France	Finland	United Kingdom

Hopefully, this chapter will help put into perspective where the largest revenue opportunities are for teen marketers on a global basis. We all have impressions of where there are strong consumer-oriented economies and where there are big populations. But before this data became available, marketers were not able to put together teen spending intensity with the size of the teen population, factoring in class strata and region for an apples-to-apples comparison.

From this analysis we can identify what I call the *$1 Billion Club*—that is, countries where annual teen spending is reported to be $1 billion or more. What first has to be taken into consideration is that the United States represents almost one-fourth of all teen spending worldwide. India, which may surprise some, is second, and Brazil is third.

The $1 Billion Club

Markets Where Teen Spending Exceeds $1 Billion

Country	$ Billions	Country	$ Billions
United States	27	France	3
India	16	Mexico	3
Brazil	15	Colombia	2
Japan	7	Philippines	2
Germany	6	South Africa	2
Argentina	5	Canada	2
United Kingdom	4	Taiwan	2
Thailand	4	Spain	2
China	4	Australia	1
Russia	3	Poland	1
South Korea	3		

Honorable Mentions: Markets Where Teen Spending Exceeds $750 Million

Country	$ Millions	Country	$ Millions
Netherlands	952	Peru	781
Sweden	870	Greece	759

Note: See the Appendix for detailed tables.

These estimates are intentionally on the low side, because I chose to play it safe. Any upside potential is gravy for marketers. Remember that there are types of teen spending that are not accounted for in these estimates of what teens spend and control directly. It does not account for all the money spent on teens by parents, grandparents, and others for clothes, food, entertainment, electronics and

computer technology, education, or travel. Hence, it is not an estimate of the teen market for goods and services—only of what teens
themselves spend. What we are looking at here is what kind of
money passes through teens' own hands with direct control.

It also does not account for a factor that probably quadruples
teens' spending influence—for instance, telling parents what car
to buy, where to vacation this year, and what stereo system to put
in the den. Teens serve the role of opinion leaders, and even
experts, in their families in many categories worldwide—especially in electronics and technology.

Third, this estimate does not take into account the power of
youth spending among young teens and preteens below 15 years of
age, or spending among slightly older cohorts over age 19. Again,
I believe this would be a multiplying factor of great significance.

What this data does enable us to do is put the world in relative
perspective from a teen revenue resource standpoint. While most
teen marketers consider the United States to be very important to
the mix, few marketers consider the full potential of India or
Brazil, which rank second and third respectively in billions of dollars spent annually by teens.

In her book *Snakes and Ladders* (Anchor Books, 1997), journal-
ist Gita Mehta reports a banker's estimate of 20 million million-
aires in India. When most Westerners think of India, they see a sea
of poverty. Certainly, that large segment of the huge India population still exists. But more obscure to the foreign eye is the deep
cluster of wealth that exists and is growing in modern-day India.
This wealth extends to the upper-middle-class youth who are both
sophisticated and cosmopolitan. In Chapter 7 there is a snapshot
of Indian youth culture that addresses what makes teen youth culture there unique. There are some hurdles for foreign marketers
because of an historical push to nationalize industries. However,
opportunities appear to be growing for external marketers, and the
market is worth pursuing given that it is the largest teen market in
the world in terms of population numbers.

Economic targeting also takes on a different character when youth spending potential is evaluated on a regional basis. Here is how the various regions stack up:

Annual Teen Spending by Region

Asia Pacific $41 billion
North America $29 billion
South America $26 billion
Western Europe* $18 billion
Eastern Europe $4 billion
Africa[†] $2 billion

Just Say Charge It

Usually when we think of teens openly spending money, we think of cash—cold hard currency—loose change or wadded bills in the pockets of some faded Levi's. Few teens worldwide have access to a credit card—only 13 percent, on average. However, on a country-by-country basis, the role of plastic payment varies radically.

In the United States, 1 in 5 teens is able to access a credit card. The same is true in the United Kingdom, Brazil, and South Africa. Levels of credit card usage are highest in France, Norway, and Belgium, which tops the list at more than half of all teens (56 percent). This suggests that in these high-incidence countries, bigger-ticket items and brand choices are likely to be directly controlled by teens because the ceiling on the amount spent for a given transaction may be open ended.

*Data for Italy not available.
[†]Only South Africa and Nigeria were studied.

Teen Credit Card Usage (World Average 13 Percent)

Country	Percentage	Country	Percentage
Belgium	56	Venezuela	13
Norway	46	Chile	13
France	39	Mexico	12
Turkey	35	Italy	12
Denmark	30	Hong Kong	12
Netherlands	29	Canada	11
Australia	26	India	11
Israel	25	Hungary	10
Brazil	20	Singapore	9
South Africa	20	Spain	9
United Kingdom	20	Indonesia	9
United States	20	Latvia	7
Finland	17	Greece	6
Taiwan	16	China	5
Colombia	16	Peru	5
Argentina	16	Japan	4
Sweden	16	Poland	4
Estonia	15	Russia	4
Germany	15	Lithuania	4
Philippines	15	Nigeria	3
South Korea	15	Ukraine	1
Thailand	14	Vietnam	1

Why Only One Brand Will Do

Part of what drives the flow of money among youth is the insistence that product purchases be for the right brands. Because young people's identity is so tentative, having the right brands is a way of telegraphically belonging to the right group.

It is therefore somewhat ironic that the teens who are most concerned about wearing the right brands come from both the economically challenged nations (Indonesia, India, and Nigeria)

Teens Who Say There Are Things They Won't Wear or Use If They're Not the Right Brand (World Average 26 Percent)

Country	Percentage	Country	Percentage
Indonesia	62	Colombia	23
India	45	Norway	23
Nigeria	44	Germany	23
United Kingdom	43	Taiwan	22
United States	40	Turkey	21
Ukraine	35	Netherlands	21
Latvia	34	Greece	20
Canada	33	Singapore	19
Australia	32	Mexico	19
Vietnam	30	Poland	18
South Africa	30	Lithuania	17
Philippines	30	Spain	17
South Korea	29	Denmark	17
Peru	28	Japan	17
Russia	26	Venezuela	17
Sweden	26	Italy	16
Hungary	25	Chile	16
Estonia	25	Argentina	15
Thailand	25	China	13
Israel	25	Brazil	13
Finland	24	France	10
Hong Kong	24	Belgium	9

and two of the world's richest (the United Kingdom and the United States).

Also ironic is that both France and China are among the weakest in concern for fashion brand correctness. France is traditionally considered one of the fashion capitals of the world. And yet, it is also characterized by proud individualism. The Chinese, by contrast, are just discovering brands and are far less knowledgeable about the statements they make. I predict these feelings are likely to change in China in the near future.

It's Only Money

A corollary to the attitude of not settling for a nonpreferred apparel brand is a sentiment that cuts across multiple product categories, expressed by the attitude, "When I really want a brand, price doesn't matter." This is a somewhat cavalier attitude among a huge population that is largely not self-supporting. However, the passion for brand correctness runs deep. The list of countries that score high on this orientation is astonishing because it spans countries that suffer economically as well as those that epitomize consumer culture—the United States and Japan.

Teens Who Say Price Doesn't Matter When They Really Want a Brand (World Average 24 Percent)

Country	Percentage	Country	Percentage
India	39	South Africa	24
Australia	37	Indonesia	24
Lithuania	36	Latvia	24
Japan	36	Netherlands	23
South Korea	36	Brazil	23
United States	34	Sweden	23
Canada	33	Taiwan	22
Thailand	32	Hungary	21
Turkey	31	Singapore	20
Vietnam	31	Poland	18
Philippines	31	France	18
Ukraine	31	China	17
Greece	30	Norway	17
Germany	30	Finland	16
United Kingdom	29	Hong Kong	16
Estonia	28	Italy	16
Nigeria	28	Denmark	14
Israel	26	Belgium	13
Russia	25		

What this means is that the power of brand equity is a global phenomenon that translates to price value. It also means that the next generation discriminates as shoppers, understands brand benefits, and won't be talked down when its heart is set on having what it perceives as the best.

This, of course, is what marketers strive for. To have firm preference and brand loyalty is what builds global leadership brands. Most likely, this attitude varies by category. When a kid craves a Mars bar, it is likely that nothing else will do. The same may go for the right jeans or the most popular style of backpack. But on a big-ticket item such as a computer, the reality is that price may more often be the ultimate tiebreaker.

Slow Down the Flow

What is more surprising is the intensity with which global youth is saving money! Often this reflects short-term savings for big-ticket items such as leather jackets, sound systems, and so on. In the United States, many teens save to buy their first car or raise money for car insurance.

Also, where money is required to pay for college, as it is in the United States, teens are often expected to start amassing their own funds. For many youths, a self-funded education is the only ticket to the dream fulfillment they seek for a comfortable adult life.

Perhaps financial services companies should take note and consider approaching the market at a younger point of entry. First of all, youths would benefit from the invaluable financial planning habits. Second, savvy planning would help ease the future, and they would develop an important relationship that would be likely to grow with increased age and wealth. The information in the

Teens Who Are Saving Money for the Future (World Average 37 Percent)

Country	Percentage	Country	Percentage
Indonesia	72	Mexico	38
Netherlands	61	France	37
Thailand	61	Peru	37
Belgium	60	Israel	35
Hong Kong	59	China	35
Australia	58	Norway	35
United Kingdom	57	Sweden	34
Philippines	56	South Korea	33
United States	53	Chile	32
Colombia	53	Hungary	31
Canada	52	Greece	30
Taiwan	52	Lithuania	26
South Africa	47	Turkey	25
Singapore	46	Japan	24
Spain	44	Poland	24
Denmark	44	Brazil	24
Venezuela	42	Vietnam	20
Argentina	42	Estonia	18
India	41	Ukraine	16
Nigeria	41	Latvia	16
Italy	39	Russia	14
Finland	38	Germany	12

table will help the stock brokerages and investment houses know where to target youth products.

When I was growing up in the Midwest, it was common for kids to put their extra allowance, babysitting, and paper route money into a Christmas fund at the bank. After saving all year, they would have money to buy Christmas presents. The same could be established for funding higher education, or even vesting capital for entrepreneurship.

Occasional Windfalls

Usually when we think of teens saving money, we think of small amounts. There is the money from birthday, holiday, and graduation gifts; small sums earned for day chores; amassed allowance; or savings from (most likely) minimum-wage after-school, weekend, and summer jobs.

However, there is that small group of teens—mostly in the United States—who become financial heroes for the generation. There are the Internet whiz kids, the rap singers with golden voices, and the Hollywood young elite, who make money at levels beyond most adult dreams.

While every generation has had its exceptions, this generation is different in the access that young people have to really *big* money based on their own talent and initiative. In part, this is because today's youth lives on the cutting edge of technology and is most comfortable resting on its applications. Business has therefore sought out this talent. It is also because youth has become such a big target market, particularly for the music and movie industries, that it is also needed as talent to fuel the business.

Every day there are stories in the U.S. news about young people making big money. Just today I read in the *San Jose Mercury News* (from the Yahoo! Web site) about Hans Pang, a 17-year-old California high school student who worked this summer for a hot Silicon Valley start-up and saw the value of his stock options soar to more than $100,000. Instead of salary, this smart young self-navigator agreed to accept an option of 750 shares. Then the stock went public, and the value of his stake soared. What a good learning experience that summer job was! Financial service providers should be thinking young!

In sum, today's global youth generation stands for big money. This is reflected in the money youths physically control, the purchasing power they have in influencing family members, and the ultimate earning potential that sometimes comes fast and big, as it did for young Hans Pang.

The other beautiful part about this target from a marketer's perspective is that growing minds are fresh, open, and fair. They are not mired in 20-plus years of brand habits, as most boomers are. Consequently, if a marketer can make an honest value proposition that makes sense to this young market group, success is probable. The rest of this book tells you how to start.

3

The 10 Unifiers of
Global Youth Culture

Global teens share much in common. And what they share are
similar threads that connect almost all teens to each other. I
call these threads *unifiers*. The unifiers are the pillars, the shared
beliefs, on which global teen culture rests. Extensive research
reveals that there are 10 unifiers that are common to all teens.

It is important for marketers to understand these 10 unifiers in
order to consider strategies for promotion and advertising. Why?
Because insights into what makes teens the same globally can create a single marketing strategy that works everywhere.

The best way to build a global brand position for teens is to
leverage one of the unifiers of teen culture. These unifiers were
identified by quantitative research and illuminated by thousands
of conversations. A unifier is a common chord that resounds to the
heart of group connection. Unifiers reflect shared interests,
beliefs, and values. Together they comprise the sum of what makes
up a unified culture.

Unifiers, in essence, create a unique toolbox for marketers to draw upon in establishing brand values, brand personality, and brand relevance to a generation. The unifiers are shortcuts to immediacy and relevance. They are limited only by marketing imagination for ad themes, promotions, sponsorships, and style.

Finding the right insight into what makes teens the same globally, marketers can create a single marketing strategy that works everywhere. The result is the creation and reinforcement of a global brand with significant cost efficiencies.

Michael Jordan for Nike is a brilliant example. As the most admired sports figure worldwide, he embodies the essence of far-reaching greatness that is synonymous with the athletic footwear's "Just Do It" positioning. Utilizing the worldwide recognition and admiration of Michael Jordan leverages a core unifier for the brand's growth and continued success.

Another example is the current achievement of the global Royal Philips Electronics campaign. The power of the Philips "Let's Make Things Better" theme plays directly to the three unifiers of self-navigation, hope and trust in the future, and passion for technology, as listed in the following section.

The 10 Unifiers: A Marketer's Toolbox

Once you understand that the global teen represents billions in potential revenue, the most important fact to learn from this book is what the unifiers are and how to use them successfully in marketing campaigns.

The unifiers represent the pillars of the new youth culture. Some are values. Some are affinities or interests. Most are a combination of both. Few will change in this cohort's lifetime. These are the reasons why these unifiers are so valuable.

Most teen marketers keep their radar out for current fads and fashions. Some may hire such excellent trend watchers and youth consultants as Marian Salzman or Irma Zandel. Some companies are smart enough to consult with kids themselves to tell them what's hot and what's not. I have found that if a marketing program is not tied to a fundamental unifier—one that provides an enduring foundation—then every six months marketers will be doomed to rediscover or to guess at what's in. This is because fads, fashions, and interests are as changeable as the weather. They do not endure.

On the other hand, if a marketer can link a brand to one or more global unifiers, then the current pop cultural references become frosting on the cake. What makes the teens of this generation so unique is the fact that they can be treated as a global target because they share a common, unwavering foundation of beliefs and interests.

For marketers, these 10 unifiers are also guidelines. Any one or two can build a brand. The 10 unifiers of global youth culture are as follows:

1. *Unabashed consumerism*
2. *Passion for technology*
3. *Perpetual entertainment*
4. *Endless experience and learning*
5. *Exploration and mobility*
6. *Sports participation and observation*
7. *Respect for global icons*
8. *Humanism and empathy*
9. *Hope and trust in the future*
10. *Self-navigation—the ultimate unifier*

Unifier 1: Unabashed Consumerism

In an age of abundance for much of the world's growing middle class, teens see consumer products as one of the limitless joys of life.

Affluent lifestyles are portrayed in lush detail on internationally syndicated shows like *Beverly Hills 90210*, *Baywatch*, and *Friends*. Hollywood movies portray the availability of million-dollar homes, sports cars, designer clothes, and state-of-the-art electronics.

Advertising is everywhere, with 81 percent of teens worldwide watching approximately 2 hours of television daily. The malls in Sydney, São Paulo, Singapore, Hong Kong, and now even Shanghai are filled with a full array of products. Consumer goods are everywhere, and today's youth generation aspires to own as much as it can as soon as it can. Since almost all global teens have access to some cash, either from paying jobs or from allowances, they have become budding consumers with brand preferences.

The first table shows just a portion of what teens are expected to pay for with their own money. There is also a huge global penetration of consumer goods that teens already own or use, as the second table shows. It is no wonder that the number-one concern among teens worldwide is getting a good job. This is because the power to buy consumer goods is the ultimate challenge that teens will face in the future.

Some marketing critics will find this unifier of consumerism somewhat disappointing. They may ponder whatever happened to the idealism of youth. The fact is that today's youth are wise beyond their years when it comes to idealism. Moreover they are pragmatic and perceive the economic reality of empowerment.

Purchases Teens Make with Their Own Money

Product	United States	Western Europe	China	India	Latin America
Food/snacks	51%	37%	63%	63%	24%
Beverages	45	35	52	41	22
CDs/tapes	54	49	23	27	14
Movies	41	37	17	35	15
Clothing	41	35	22	30	14
Cosmetics	24	23	5	22	8
Film	13	12	4	17	4

Global Penetration of Consumer Goods Owned by Teens

Product	Percentage	Product	Percentage
Blue jeans	91	Blazer	52
Wristwatch	91	Flannel shirt	51
Athletic shoes	88	Hair gel/mousse	46
T-shirt	87	Earrings	44
Perfume/cologne	70	Outdoor/hiking boots	43
Backpack	66	Denim jacket	41
Antiperspirant/deodorant	65	Hairspray	40
Good suit/dress	62	College sweatshirt/T-shirt	38

The aspiration for financial success is the motivation that leads youth to good-paying jobs and the ability to buy goods. These teens also expect that money will buy them the time and freedom to pursue the nonmaterial treasures that life has to offer.

This teen hunger and sense of the possibility of controlling their own destiny is what I call *self-navigation*. The global self-navigators are practical yet motivated to get goods through their own hard work, ambition, and wits.

Even in less developed countries, teens manage to find money to purchase products, even if that means convincing their parents to pay. Visit Caracas and see the teens carrying cellular phones, or walk through Bangkok and observe the $150 Adidas, or stop in Moscow and notice all the $100 Levi's. These are mostly parental purchases.

Unifier 2: Passion for Technology

Technology is what makes today's global youth culture possible. Through television, media, and computers there has been an ongoing cultural exchange that is uniform in its impact on these global teens.

Technology is the epitome of what makes this next generation so special. Learning computers in the classroom, as many do throughout the world, teens have leapfrogged over their parents in understanding the ways and means of information access and e-commerce. Moreover, technology has broadened these teens' view of the world and hastened their infinite abilities to connect to it.

This generation feels no ambivalence about technology, as older generations did. These kids find it easy to master and enjoy technology. Teens the world over envision technological advancements as both a creator of new jobs and a conduit to a better way of life. Technology is the yellow brick road that will lead to the land of tomorrow's prosperous future. And remember, these kids want to be prosperous.

When global teens think about the inherent values of technology, they state with enthusiasm that technological products "will help me to get ahead," "will make my job easier," and "will help me be more efficient on the job."

Technology also supplies an additional benefit for this fast-paced pleasure-seeking generation: It frees teens from boring tasks. These kids understand the fun aspect of technology, especially computers. For many, computer games were their first experience with computers. Technology offers a faster roller-coaster ride to the future, with more thrills.

Here's an additional key point: The more technology teens have, the more they want. It's a little like the famous Lay's Potato Chips campaign: "I'll bet you can't eat just one bite of technology." And teens can't. They are voracious technological consumers. This means their loyalty is to the new, to the improved, to the device that is faster, with more bells and whistles. Marketers in the electronics industry have discovered that if you build it better, teens will be the first to find it.

Teens see only the upside to technology and do not experience any sense of loss about leaving traditions behind. This creates a division between generations, a generation gap in which teens advance with technology, potentially leaving the older generation behind. In the United States, there is a widespread phenomenon of grandparents communicating with grandchildren via e-mail on the computer or Web TV simply because they have learned how to operate e-mail from their grandkids.

Nonetheless, the technology transfer across generations works both ways. Many upscale youth in developed countries are conversant with computer communications and entertainment technology because they have had access and skills passed along by their parents.

In less-developed countries, technological access is more likely to come from the schools. This is why, much to my initial amazement, I measured higher computer usage among teens in developing nations like Peru than in highly developed Japan.

Poorer countries are among the first to recognize that technological training will potentially level the worldwide economic playing field. Disparity in levels of access to technology is actually one of the great differentiators of youth culture because, as shown by the examples that follow, access is not evenly available throughout the world. What remains as a dominant unifier of global youth, however, is its universal passion to embrace the new and the possible.

Many parents of young children worry about their kids playing video and computer games for hour after hour. I believe that these games develop important skills for the next generation of technology users, much like learning the alphabet. What kids get out of early electronic games is an adeptness at hand-eye coordination that will be invaluable later on. They also learn to think with technological logic, becoming able to almost intuit how things work. Dealing with high-speed sensory stimuli and multitasking—these are essential skills that only this new generation has mastered, as will those that will follow.

I was amazed when my daughter Emily, then age 11, was able to hook up our new color printer by talking to her friend online and "rooting around" to make it work. Her communications on the Internet even then were almost as seamless as those of any of my computer-savvy colleagues. Learning computers and technology is much the same as learning a new language. Conventional wisdom says start young.

It should also be noted that the passion for technology goes way beyond computers. For this new generation of consumers, technology equals not just functionality but fun. Avid mediavores, young people throughout the world are enamored with devices that provide entertainment and keep them connected to each other. This means that televisions, stereos, digital video discs (DVDs), cellular phones, and pagers are all high on the I-got-to-have-it list.

In one study I did for Philips, I was astounded that kids not only asked for electronics gifts by brand name, but they also specified the style and model number. As smart consumers, young people learn markets in depth and discriminate on the finest details.

It also fascinates me that retailers who want to look hip to youth, such as Nike, Levi's, and Diesel, use electronics prominently in their stores via video walls and surround-sound music. These signal to the teen generation that the store is a happening place and the products sold inside are current and cool.

The world of youth is marked by sensory electronic stimulation. Any marketer who wants to connect with this generation should consider the leverage potential in electronics and technology. This can include the presentation of information on Internet sites, electronics sweepstakes, and even the final sale through e-commerce. Make no mistake—youth is electronic.

Unifier 3: Perpetual Entertainment

When Cindy Lauper sings "Girls Just Wanna Have Fun," I think of the whole new world youth generation. While it would be a serious disservice to this wonderful, mature-beyond-their-years cohort to suggest that *all* they want to do is have fun, it should never be forgotten that pleasure is a serious driver. Not so far removed from childhood, with a natural life-stage bent toward playfulness, today's youths have an insatiable appetite for ubiquitous entertainment.

Music goes with them. Games go with them. Soon video will go along as well. Royal Philips Electronics is even developing electronic clothing with all kinds of potential pleasures, including speakers built into the hood of a jacket for perfect surround sound.

When I think of teens, I imagine constant movement and stimulation. Much of this stimulation comes from an addiction to media in every form, enabled by technology. Playing video games, talking on the phone, working on the computer, watching MTV—these tasks can all be accomplished simultaneously by the typical teenager.

When I ran BrainWaves, I had several young adults working on computers with data and graphics. Even then, I could not fathom how their work could be so good with loud music in the background and when they were always on the phone as they were working. Nonetheless, I have never been one to challenge quality results.

The list of what teens like to do for entertainment throughout the world is wide and long. First and foremost, they are *mediavores*, needing to be fed healthy doses of daily television, radio, magazines, newspapers, and news. With the world moving so fast and change occurring at the speed of light, the proverbial question "What's happening?" is expected to be answered with significance.

Beyond television, movies and music feed an insatiable thirst. Going to the movies, renting movies, watching movies on videotape or DVD, listening to CDs, making their own tapes and CDs, and now downloading music over the Internet makes the stream of entertainment constant, satisfying, and affordable.

Teens participate on the cutting edge of culture by keeping their antennae out. This means that it won't be difficult for marketers to be heard or seen. The other good news is that media access is almost simultaneous. Cable television and satellite dishes make it possible for teens to see MTV and other youth-directed programming almost everywhere at the same time.

Overnight, programs and advertisers can broadcast messages to millions of teens. Event marketing is also capable of creating a ripple through the global teens, as recently occurred with the release of the latest Star Wars film, *The Phantom Menace*. No longer do time and space barriers exist between what is broadcast or released in the United States, or anywhere else, and what is received abroad.

In addition to the obvious media involvement, youths find fun through a number of varied activities. Many are social—spending time with friends, talking on the phone and going to parties. Others are sometimes more solitary—taking photos, keeping a journal, or being outdoors with nature. At the core of these activities is a shared zest for life that earmarks this new generation as open and positive to all the world has to offer.

This is why ads laden with cynicism, rebellion, and negativity, based on misguided assumptions, are going to be way off the mark in succeeding with these teens.

Unifier 4: Endless Sensation and Learning

Global teens have been brought up to experience and to expect sensory stimulation. This generation is constantly looking for new thrills that entertain. The preferred music is loud. The movies enjoyed feature fast action. The dances are rhythmic and frenetic. These teens are energy in motion.

The craving for new sensations leads these teens to test their mettle and push to the extremes. They play out life to the max. Global teens have a very low threshold for boredom, and this is an essential finding for marketers: *Do not bore this generation or it will abandon you.*

The proliferation of electronic gadgetry, especially communication devices, has fostered a new class of person, the plugged-in teen. Whether they carry pagers or cellular telephones, these new global teens are in constant communication with peers. Why wait to get home to speak to a friend or classmate when they are reachable instantaneously?

Via computers and the Internet, e-mail and instant messages link one teenager with another. Graphic images and the latest music are also sent online. The computer has become a wondrous sensory fun box, generating a seemingly infinite inventory of new sensations to experience.

Out or In?

To determine how and when teens search out additional sensations is to ask whether they are in or out at night. In the United States and Europe, teens are out as often as possible. It is cool to be out, meeting pals and peers at the mall or in cafés.

In Asia, the opposite is true, because teens are at home most of the time doing homework. However, as China and Indonesia become more westernized, urban teens will want to take to the streets at night.

Technology Again

To supply teenagers with the pinnacle of sensory stimuli, the makers of television sets are developing new systems that will offer a total computer-activated technology via a user-friendly remote or voice control at greater speed than the existing telephone lines. To teens, faster, sharper, and louder have become the mantras for their generation.

With all this passion for sensation, it is therefore a relief to discover that the main part of youth stimulation is educational and harmless. While extreme sports offer a strong allure, this is not a generation that is characterized by rampant indulgence in drugs, alcohol, or sex without commitment. If anything, this new youth generation is too excited by reality and driven by the siren song of potential achievement, success, and ultimate consumerism to want to risk all for dangers.

Given this perspective, it should not be too surprising that the joy of learning is an important subset of the desire for sensation. First of all, learning is the number-one skill that this generation has mastered. It also considers the number-one job to be getting good grades.

In part, technology has made learning fun and has given this generation a more heightened sense of empowerment than any previous generation has ever had. Youths understand how to obtain what they don't know better and faster than older cohorts.

For marketers, this particular unifier can provide endless opportunities in linking experience and knowledge. A brand can benefit by offering a promotion that promises the best party anywhere on earth. But consider the lasting respect you can garner for your icon if you offer the best college education.

Unifier 5: Exploration and Mobility

Teens love to travel, and even seriously consider working in or moving to a foreign country. With the elimination of many of the historic political and economic obstacles, teens have placed international travel as a top priority. The glamour and excitement of foreign lands is no longer merely a hopeful fantasy. Teens are ready, willing, and able to get up and go.

In one sense, teens move via technology before they physically pull up stakes. Mentally, through television or the Internet, they are able to visit people and places that are many miles, if not continents, away.

If technology is leveling the playing field, then those teens who can speak software or e-commerce will be able to travel anywhere. Not only do jobs await these commercial travelers, but so do adventures.

Many teens state that they do not intend to live in the town where they were raised. The study indicates that 73 percent of global teens ultimately plan to leave their hometown after graduation. Further, only 43 percent predicted they would live in the country of their birth. Although Americans are familiar with this dispersion phenomenon, it is brand new in many countries.

Four elements characterize the mobility of teens:

- Youth has wanderlust, and the reduction in the cost of travel allows teens to act on this feeling.
- Teens have a new sense of global identity that is tied into the global marketplace and the global culture.
- In Europe, the European Union has eradicated national boundaries, so teens can now move across countries to find new jobs or better paying ones.
- A new message is being trumpeted that shouts anything is possible and you can make it happen for yourself.

For many teens in underdeveloped countries, the fear is that they will be left behind economically unless they move to the centers of commerce. Although the United States and Europe have experienced this trend in the past, the citybound migration of teens is new for Latin America and southeast Asia.

I predict that Europe will be one locus for great teen migrations in future years. The European Union has eliminated passports between countries. Moreover, European companies seeking lower labor rates will move factories south into Italy and Spain, creating jobs not only for locals but also for other Europeans looking for work. Workers will be paid the new currency of Western Europe, the euro, which is scheduled to finalize its transformation into user currency in January 2002.

To witness the commingling of thousands of teens from all over the world, visit Shaftsbury Avenue near London's West End on a warm spring or summer Saturday evening. Here, in one glance, is the outdoor meeting place of swarms of global teens that dress alike and speak English, American style. They have traveled from all over the world.

Another great locus of migration will be the United States. This is because the United States is the number-one place that teens would most like to visit or move to, outside their own countries. The reasons are plentiful. First, the United States is seen as the capital of modern culture for global teens. Second, it is considered the land of opportunity, where it is possible to make your way in the world. Third, American universities are admired for quality as well as accessibility of education. Remember that in many countries only the top students are allowed to go to university. Fourth, the United States is considered to be the center of several hot industries that appeal to youth, including general technology, computers and software, movies and media, marketing, and finance.

At the same time Asia, and especially China, offers a hotbed of opportunity for ambitious youth. This is because many new skills and talents will be welcome to assist developing countries. There are many fortunes to be made in Asia over the next 20 years, and today's youth will not miss out on this opportunity.

How can a marketer take advantage of this particular unifier? It's easy: Leverage the globalness of the brand. Sponsor trips and cultural exchanges. Put together all-star bands, teams, and game competitions. Get kids moving, and they will be forever thankful.

Unifier 6: Sports Participation and Observation

Teens love sports. This may not sound like news to you. But the wide global scale on which youth shares this enthusiasm is somewhat of a surprise. Major sporting events such as the World Cup or the National Basketball Association (NBA) finals capture the generation's eyeballs all at once. Almost every teen sees the event at the same time, creating an enormous market that an advertiser can reach with one commercial. Athletic clothes and teen logos become mainstays of the generation's wardrobe.

Perhaps the biggest news is that girls play and love sports, too. Teenage girls are becoming more involved in and more enamored with all sports. Teenage girls consider basketball their most favored sport, and they share the boys' enthusiasm for international basketball stars.

If the newly formed Women's National Basketball Association (WNBA) succeeds in attracting an audience, then girls, first in the United States and then later worldwide, will begin to have professional female basketball players as models to emulate.

Women's soccer demonstrated its appeal in last year's World Cup, held in the United States. Whether it can also build a viable league remains to be answered later. But there is the hope, especially among American teenage girls, as well as Umbro, that women's soccer will flower and realize itself.

Other Reasons

Two other factors have contributed to the success of sports as a global teen unifier: cable television and the internationalization of professional teams. Cable television, especially in the United States, has offered a wide array of all sports, including many that are less popular in this country.

A U.S. teen with cable can view live or taped Italian, English, and Mexican soccer leagues; cricket; Rugby Union and Rugby League; Australian Rules football; Irish curling and Irish football; indoor and outdoor dirt bike and motorcycle racing; National Association of Stock Car Auto Racing (NASCAR) automobile and other vehicle races; thoroughbred and trotting horse racing; track and field events; golf; college, Canadian league, and European American football; National Collegiate Athletic Association (NCAA) lacrosse, hockey, and wrestling; tennis tournaments; and even billiard pool.

In addition, professional sports teams in soccer, basketball, and hockey are dipping into an international pool of talent and breaking down the barriers of nationalism. In the past, if you were a soccer player from Brazil, you played in Brazil. Now you play for Manchester United in the United Kingdom along with other players, about 30 percent of who come from countries other than Great Britain.

The internationalization of sports means that a teen in the Ukraine will root for the New York Rangers because his hometown hero plays ice hockey for that club. Likewise, a teen from the Dominican Republic will root for the Chicago Cubs because of slugger Sammy Sosa. Alternatively, a teen from Bangor, Maine, will root for the Barcelona Dragons in the European professional football league because his local college hero from the University of Maine plays in that league.

NBA All the Way

The most savvy of all professional leagues is the NBA, which has parlayed the fast pace of its sport, the superhero status of Michael Jordan, and the burgeoning international availability of its players into a lucrative worldwide franchise.

The NBA conducts clinics throughout the world, sending forth its stars as ambassadors of the game. Further, it generates untold annual income via line extensions in sneakers and licensing for clothing. Colorful logos for the Chicago Bulls, the Utah Jazz, the Los Angeles Lakers, and the other NBA teams appear in every country.

Finally, sports are a great equalizer. I have seen teens in the poorest slums of Rio having a great time and making phenomenal plays with a soccer ball. My BrainWaves colleague Chip Walker has witnessed street kids in the Philippines making their own fun with makeshift basketball hoops.

Chip and I watched young Venezuelans talk about their passion for baseball. The beauty of sports is that they allow young people to challenge their own abilities while also learning the power of teamwork. Sports give youth positive heroes. They provide examples of people, rich or poor of any race, who through their own dedication and talent can beat the odds to become famous, successful, and a source of pride to family and country.

Sports break down the barriers of geography and connect them on a positive, human level. This is why it is so important to identify sports as one of the unifiers of global teen culture.

Unifier 7: Respect for Global Icons

Teens desire the known advertised brands and well-known consumer goods because these become an individual's identity statement. They proclaim to the world that the teen is a player and a person to be respected for what he or she can attain. In essence, consumer goods become talismans of image creation. The teen says, "I consume, therefore I am."

The awareness of top international brands is so high among teens that their logos have become global icons. Teens around the world recognize the logos of Coca-Cola, Pepsi, Sony, Adidas, and even IBM.

Sometimes the power of a global brand icon comes from early imprinting, as with Colgate and Johnson & Johnson, which rank sixth and tenth out of 75 icons tested. These are not necessarily teen brands in the true sense of being mainly for teens. And yet, due to consistent exposure and positioning, these two brands have developed a firm and friendly grounding in the minds of today's youth.

Other brands, like Coca-Cola and Adidas, are considered primarily youth-oriented, and yet they face a different set of challenges. It is imperative for these brands to reconnect with each new generation as it enters the marketplace. Icon status has to be earned and won with each new generation. The established leader that forgets this lesson is doomed to lose market share.

Perhaps the most interesting of the global icons are the new and unexpected. Who would have expected the Chicago Bulls logo to have higher recognition status than Levi's, or even the Olympic rings? The significance of the Bulls' rapid rise is that meaningful brands with relevance to a generation can be catapulted to world icon status in a relatively short time—if the marketing and the image are right.

Hence, some of these brands are old institutions and some are relatively newer to the radar screen—MTV, CNN, and Nintendo.

Why is respect for global icons given unifier status? It is because they represent a common language for the new global culture. These icons embody more than products. Disney stands for wonder and delight. Kodak represents memories. Coca-Cola symbolizes refreshment. And Philips speaks to hope through innovation.

These brand names and logos have tremendous symbolic value. They have equity that plays to Wall Street, and they represent a friendly, reliable face in a sea of consumer goods.

Another point about global icons is that today's global youth really admires successful marketers. Having been exposed to marketing campaigns since infancy, teens understand segment targeting, media expenditures, and promotional programs with the savvy of a marketing consultant.

I have been astounded many times when leading focus groups among teens who speak the marketing lexicon as well as my clients. "Who is the target for the ad?" they often ask. "Because if it's me, then. . . ."

As a unifier, achieving global brand icon status is a goal for many brands. Maintaining global brand icon status is also a goal for others.

The groundbreaking work done by D'Arcy on brand leadership worldwide indicates that leadership icons carry a multitude of positive image associations. If a brand is considered a leader in its category, then it has about an 80 percent chance of also being considered high quality, good value, reliable, and trustworthy.

To be a global icon means to have strongly rooted trust for important aspects that go way beyond recognition of the symbol itself.

Let's say you are marketing a brand with broad international distribution but that has not reached icon status. What can you do? How can you leverage this global unifier? While this topic is more fully advanced in Chapter 9, the short answer is: Create opportunities to align with other major players in noncompetitive categories. Study their marketing programs. Examine their advertising. There is much to be learned from the giants who do it right.

Unifier 8: Humanism and Empathy

I sometimes feel like a mama bear defending the generation to cynical adults who assume the worst in everyone, especially teens. But the truth is that teenagers the world over do not need to be defended as much as they need to be recognized for being innately good and caring human beings.

The evidence comes from several directions. The first is in the area of personal relationships. Of all teens' guiding principles, the one that is most prevalent is the importance they place on their relationships with their families above all else.

Note that the relationship with friends ranks as the number-three driving principle. Parents and friends are both critical to almost any teen's world. Next to getting a good job, worry about parents' health is the number-2 worry out of 46 items rated. More-

Driving Principles of Highest Importance to Teens

Principle	Percentage
Relationship with family	56
Accomplishing as much as I can	46
My relationships with friends	42
Having as much fun as I can	34
Having the power and influence to get what I want in life	29
Being accepted as an individual	28
Making the world a better place	26
Never being bored	25
Fitting into society	22
Upholding time-honored traditions, customs, and values	12

over, spending time with friends ranked third, at 77 percent out of almost 50 possible activities for enjoyment, next to listening to tapes and CDs (number 1), and watching television (number 2).

Probably the high involvement with friends comes as no surprise. But families? Almost half of the teens (44 percent) say they *enjoy* spending time with their families. This really isn't so shocking. Many teenage kids still have great times with their families—watching sports, going to movies, taking family vacations, and so on. In many parts of the world, extended family and friends are one, with cousins serving as best friends. But what about parents specifically? The majority of teens throughout the world (79 percent) trust their parents more than anyone else—more than their friends (66 percent), girlfriend or boyfriend (37 percent), teachers (29 percent), religious leaders (19 percent), or political leaders (4 percent).

This is a major sea change for this new generation of youth. Unlike in the past, when anyone over 30 was not to be trusted, this new cohort is far more committed to believing in the people close to them, starting with their parents.

Today's teens are neither selfish nor self-centered. As culture becomes unified it is perhaps easier for teens to have empathy and feel connected with others the world over.

Remember the international teen-oriented campaign, "The United Colors of Benetton"? Beautiful faces of all colors and ethnicities smiled at the reader, proclaiming their unity. This is a prime example of leveraging a unifier for brand positioning. But then the campaign got out of hand. Subsequent ads addressed social issues, such as people dying of AIDS. Personally, the theme ads were too morose for my taste, and I believe they were a bit of a downer for a generation that gravitates toward optimism. Not to be overly critical, but I believe that many teens rejected the ads because of what seemed like borrowed or exploited interest. If only the ads had been more hopeful, they might have achieved the desired effect. Perhaps some of the proceeds from the AIDS ad should have gone to research for AIDS, giving a sense of relevance to the connection between the brand and the advertising theme. Now, *that* would have made sense.

Teens today have achieved a natural balance by looking inward to protect and grow their own interests as well as being receptive to the needs and concerns of others. High on the concern list are AIDS, poverty, the environment, racism, terrorism, war, and world peace. Half of all teens say they hope to be able to help make the world a better place and 1 in 4 (26 percent) put their time where their mouth is through volunteer work.

Another theme that is central to this unifier is the generation's love of freedom. With historical boundaries down for travel, employment, and information, teens feel collectively that the world is theirs to enjoy, but must necessarily be shared.

I am heartened by this powerful effect of a unified global youth culture. As teens recognize their similarities the world over, it may become increasingly hard to view other nationalities as the enemy, as has been the case throughout human history.

Unifier 9: Hope and Trust in the Future

Part of teens' rampant consumerism is based on this global unifier. Two out of three teens (69 percent) expect to always have enough money to live comfortably. This perception is most pronounced in the United States, but is almost equally high in the two African countries studied. The greatest doubt is in Japan, where inflation and a slowing economy make future prospects relatively dim. In China, expectations are also relatively low. This is perhaps because they have witnessed the effects of the sudden Cultural Revolution on their parents' generation and feel uncertain about their own futures.

Perhaps as a result of these high economic expectations and a passion for having consumer goods now, few teens—only 37 percent globally—are saving money for the future.

Teens' Expectations to Have Money to Live Comfortably

Country	Percentage	Country	Percentage
United States	90	Asia Pacific	64
Africa	83	Eastern Europe	64
Western Europe	75	India	63
Latin America	74	China	48
Middle East	66	Japan	45

While economic prospects may pose some uncertainties, there are still wonderful expectations that are shared by the generation en masse that make hope a true global unifier. Consider the following list:

Teens' Expectations for the Future

Complete my education	86 percent
Have a job I like	82 percent
Succeed in my career	81 percent
Be a happy adult	79 percent
Be a healthy adult	75 percent
Have a nice house or apartment	73 percent
Have money to live comfortably	72 percent
Have my family be proud of me	70 percent
Get married	69 percent
Live in a world of peace	66 percent
Own a nice car	64 percent
Have children	63 percent

What ranks low? Two interesting contrasts of conformity and the lack thereof:

Be a rebel	13 percent
Be a part of government	12 percent

Unifier 10: Self-Navigation—The Ultimate Unifier

If I had to pick one characteristic of new world youth that is most poignant, it would be the universal belief in self-navigation. Almost everyone in our Wave II sample of 27,600 teens throughout 44 countries agreed with the statement, "It is up to me to get what I want out of life."

This is striking to me for two reasons. First, as a researcher, it is unusual to see such unanimity across such a large data set. Second,

Teens Who Agree It Is up to Them to Get What They Want out of Life (Global Average 85 Percent)

Country	Percentage	Country	Percentage
Finland	95	Argentina	87
Estonia	93	Israel	87
Venezuela	93	Spain	85
United States	93	Italy	85
Colombia	93	Brazil	84
Poland	93	Greece	84
United Kingdom	92	Lithuania	83
China	91	Nigeria	82
Thailand	91	India	80
Mexico	91	Turkey	77
Chile	90	Singapore	77
South Africa	90	Canada	76
Germany	90	Japan	76
Australia	89	Sweden	76
South Korea	89	Hong Kong	73
Norway	89	Vietnam	72
Taiwan	89	Hungary	69
Ukraine	89	Philippines	69
Denmark	89	Netherlands	69
Latvia	88	Belgium	67
Peru	88	France	61
Russia	87	Indonesia	60

as a social observer, I am stunned that in Buddhist countries such as Thailand and Indonesia, where predestination is a strong religious belief, teens think that fate is largely up to them. Moreover, in countries where strong social classes preside, making it difficult to create a life for yourself that is much different from your parents', such as India and much of Western Europe, global youth is united in setting free its own expectations. The same goes for previously communist countries where fate was predetermined and everyone's lot was supposed to be the same—Russia, Czech Republic, Hungary, Poland, and so on—teens are consistent in their belief in self-determinism.

Perhaps the poet whose work best represents the essence of this generation is the Spaniard Antonio Machado, who said there is no path—you make your path as you travel.

To believe that "It's up to me to get what I want in life" means that there are no limits, only possibilities. It means that a whole new generation of world citizens is preparing to take responsibility for its own fate. It also means that there is hope and a sense of enablement to make wonderful things happen.

One thing the teens of this generation know for sure is that the world is changing rapidly around them. But they are not afraid. On the contrary, they are running toward the future with dreams of lives that are purely of their own making. This is why teens' number-one *priority* is completing their education and their number-one *worry* is getting a good job. They are simply preparing to make the future happen to their own specifications.

One other point should be noted about self-navigation. The values of teens often serve as a cultural mirror to the broader state of society at large. In essence, teens are the early adopters of mindsets and worldviews. In the 1960s it was youth's liberalism that was a precursor for human rights, racial equality, and women's equality in the workforce. Now, once again, we see a central force in self-navigation that has already begun to expand to a much broader age range.

New world teens universally believe in self-reliance.

In the United States, we conducted a survey at BrainWaves of 1,000 adults commissioned by *American Demographics* to test this hypothesis. We discovered that 1 in 4 adults (26 percent) are also self-navigators. You can see it in the boom of entrepreneurship that is sweeping the land. Adult self-navigators, much like teens, believe that only they can resolve the opposing forces of uncertainty and possibility through self-reliance. Hippies in the 1960s talked about getting back to the land. Yuppies in the new millennium are ready to get back to the self.

Summary

The 10 unifiers of global youth culture in this chapter are the most crucial aspects in understanding what the teens of this generation share in common. They also offer powerful insights for marketers who are searching for a common theme to rally a brand position or create a global advertising campaign. In Chapter 8 you will see case history examples of how the master marketers such as Coca-Cola and the NBA have put these unifiers to work.

But beware: Understanding the unifiers is only half the story. In order to get the big picture, you need to know the actual factors that keep this generation from being completely homogenous. These are the global teen *differentiators* described in the next chapter.

4

The Key Differentiators of Global Youth: Why It's Dangerous to Generalize

In the last chapter I presented the 10 *unifiers* that influence global teens, and in this chapter I point out the key *differentiators*. To ignore these differentiators is to court disaster in developing global marketing efforts to teens.

While a teen in Beijing and a teen in Boston may have much in common—and may even dress identically—when it comes to dating, drugs, Internet usage, and, more important, attitudes about self and society, these teens are as different as night and day. Many American or European teens strive for some form of individuality to stand out from the crowd. Most Asian teens tend to consider themselves as fish in the collective shoal.

Understanding the essential differentiators that exist between teens in various countries of the world—and, often, the differences among them within countries—will have a major impact on the effectiveness of advertising and marketing programs. The importance of these differentiators to global companies is that the same message will not always appeal to every teen every time. It is crucial for marketers first to learn, and then to practice, cultural sensitivity, especially when targeting impressionable and excitable teens.

While the unifiers in the preceding chapter give marketers inspiration on how to create a brand's global positioning, it is the differentiators that should be regarded as "watch outs"—the red flags of caution. The reason I call them *watch outs* is that differentiators are the essential factors that can deter the effectiveness of a global campaign. Differentiators are the forks in the road that occur in unfamiliar terrain and can detour your communication efforts.

Do not be afraid. If you consider the differentiators a well-marked road map, you can adjust your route when necessary to allow for smooth travel.

Another analogy is to think of the differentiators as filters for marketing efforts. Analyze communication against these filters and adjust or research locally where there appears to be an incongruous fit.

If marketers apply the discipline of evaluating international marketing programs against the backdrop of these differentiators, they can proceed with confidence and avoid the vicious cycle of failure.

Differentiators are what keep the global youth target from being completely homogeneous. They are the critical factors of local realities and resulting values that can cause two teens—who essentially look and act alike—to be significantly different, particularly in the way they react to advertising.

Humor, sex, and irreverence may play well with American and European teens, but Asian teenagers might consider these same variables disrespectful, embarrassing, and in bad taste. Sometimes when I tell clients this fact, I fear they think I am imposing my own moral filters. This is not the case. I am merely trying to prevent marketers from making costly mistakes.

The most serious error for marketers is to use the lowest-common-denominator rule. This will lead to thinking of teens as irreverent, disobedient, oversexed, or sophomoric. In truth, most of them are none of these.

Eight Differentiators—Overview

There are eight important differentiators that exist among global teens. These are useful for marketers in brand positioning, advertising, promotions and sponsorships. It is also imperative to note that *values* represent the ultimate differentiator that defines all teens. The eight are as follows:

1. *Local economic realities*
2. *Worries*
3. *Love and sex*
4. *Drugs and drinking*
5. *Technological access*
6. *Responsibilities and pressures*
7. *Local pride*
8. *Values*

Differentiator 1: Local Economic Realities

All teen life has an important local component. It is the most familiar and personal tier of the dual cultural passport. These local realities dictate the lifetime economic prospects of teens. A country's trade balances, currency fluctuations, and economic development activity will impact on the job and career opportunities for teens.

Much to my delight, many young people around the world have hopeful expectations. Many teenagers in emerging and less developed countries are optimistic for a better future. Teens express an unwavering economic confidence that the world offers them a promise of material success.

Global teens are excited about their commercial prospects. They see a rapidly expanding global economy, offering many opportunities for growth. Countries in Latin America and Southeast Asia enjoy a spirit of renewed economic opportunity. Many teens in the United States and in some countries of Europe are eager to hitch their wagons to the ever-brightening technology star.

Clouds over Western Europe

I discovered one disturbing note among Western European teens. Basically, these teens are not confident that the local economy will get better in their lifetime. Their pessimistic attitude presupposes that they will not even enjoy the same good lifestyle as their parents.

This Western European negativism is surprising and, at the same time, important for marketers to understand. These teens envision a loss of state benefits and are fearful that they will have to pay for many of the expensive basics (e.g., health, housing, and education) that life under capitalistic socialism has historically afforded.

Part of the problem in Western Europe is the prevalence of a social and educational class system still governed by the old boys network. The narrow and hierarchical pyramid of education offers promising futures only to the elite students, such as those entering Oxbridge or *Ecole Supérieure*. These privileged few, like their parents, will go on to become the leaders of England and France, and of international commerce.

It should also be noted that senior job prospects for European women are few and far between. Despite important historical exceptions, such as Margaret Thatcher and Coco Chanel, it is far more a man's world in Europe than in the United States and many parts of Asia, such as Hong Kong and Singapore. I am personally grateful that I developed a thick skin before venturing into the European business world.

Another important reason for the low level of optimism in Western Europe is the lack of European Union tax incentives for entrepreneurs. It is difficult to be young and have a dollar and a dream (make that a euro and a dream) if the governing economic entities frown on assisting emerging companies. The European Union does not offer the same individual opportunities as in the United States, especially in e-commerce—at least not yet. The net result is a more pessimistic youth population in Western Europe than anywhere else in the world.

Hope in Eastern Europe

Teens in Eastern Europe are markedly different from their Western European counterparts. They experience local economic realities as changing for the better. They are eager for Western products and technology.

When I visited Hungary and Poland, I was impressed with the can-do spirit among young people. People in their twenties are eager to convert to Western capitalism, and I was struck by how much these people resembled turn-of-the-century immigrants in America looking to work hard for a better life.

Eastern European teens ride on a roller coaster of economic events. A few years ago in Russia, it was caviar and vodka in crystal glasses, and then suddenly a depression hit with the impact of the great crash of 1929.

Poland and the Czech Republic have been the leading Eastern European countries to welcome multinational companies. The economic growth there has fostered vitality among teens who aspire for the same conspicuous consumption as their American counterparts. There will be a delayed effect in moving these former European have-nots into the ranks of haves, but that day will be hopefully coming soon.

Local economic realities are a powerful catalyst for hope or despair. A good economy fuels the easily flammable hopes and dreams of the younger generation. Rampant inflation—or, as we see now in China, rising deflation—can dampen them. Beyond aspiration, economic factors can also color a generation's outlook on life. When you are optimistic, you want to spend and enjoy life because it feels as if the money will always be there. When you are pessimistic, you may spend as well, thinking, "What does it matter, I might as well live it up while I can."

The differentiators of economic realities can play an important role in how young consumers make decisions about what they should buy and how much they should spend. If a family is having trouble making ends meet in Russia, it might splurge on candy bars for the children to bring some happiness, but it will delay buying expensive Levi's.

The first questions for marketers to ask in supporting or expanding their brands internationally are the following:

- Where does my brand fit into each nation's lifestyle economically?
- What percentage of the youth population can afford it?
- What will the product symbolize?
- Will owning or using my brand spell success, or possibly irresponsible conspicuous consumption?
- Can I leverage brand values that reinforce making a smart choice, such as quality and durability, especially where money is tight?

Differentiator 2: Worries

Global teens have worries that are both local and global. With instant access to communication, there are no secrets anymore. Teens have media access to more information than their parents ever had. Through CNN, a teen watching television in Manila is as au courant as the teen in Manhattan.

The result of the steady flow of data and news is a more informed albeit a more worried teen. Access to infinite information has resulted in shortening or eliminating the innocence of today's childhood.

A teen's local worries run the usual gamut from love and dating to crime rates and the economy. These vary significantly by country, but two worries dominate global teens: doing well in school to advance to higher education and getting a good job.

So Much to Worry About: Top 10 Global Teen Worries

1. Getting a good job	70%
2. My parents' health	63
3. Losing someone I love	57
4. Finishing my education	54
5. My own health	54
6. Getting a university degree	52
7. Not getting good grades	50
8. Not having enough money	46
9. Finding someone to love	43
10. AIDS	43

The doors to higher education in Asian countries, especially Japan, are like the choices in the old game show *Let's Make a Deal*. If Japanese students can open Door 1 (the route to college), they will have a fine economic future with a prestigious Japanese company that will often last until they retire. To fail to open Door 1, and to go through Door 2 (the no-college path), is to be limited to a career in the working class, with substantially lower earning power.

A major worry of teens is having the money to buy products. Bombarded with messages from television, print, and outdoor advertising, teens have become megaconsumers.

Girls in Japan want to emulate the sophisticated Western fashion and accessory look. The peer pressure to carry a Prada bag or wear Calvin Klein clothes is powerful.

Global teens realize that a good job holds the key to unlock the doors of financial success. This pragmatic reality has produced a generation that has fewer romantics and idealists and is less rebellious than youth in former times. Today's teens have their feet planted firmly on the ground.

The worries of teens are not exclusively local, and, in fact, teens exhibit anxiety about many global problems. Teens understand that their country is just one piece of a larger economic picture. When Asia suffered its recent economic crisis, teens worldwide realized that some part of their lives would be changed by the event. Teens are very perceptive when it comes to the possible threats in the marketplace.

So while teens everywhere can share some of the same universal worries, such as getting a good job, losing someone they love, or fearing for their parents' health, it is some of the secondary worries that are dramatically differentiating.

All through Latin America, for instance, the majority of teens are worried about AIDS. Throughout most of Asia, only about 1 teen in five shares this worry.

Fear of crime is strictly a local issue. This is also a good example of why it is foolish to make generalizations about regional homogeneity. The highest concern about crime is in Asia, in Indonesia, and the lowest concern is also in Asia, in Korea, Vietnam, and Japan.

Recently, in the United States, a rash of high school shootings has made crime a widespread fear among high school students. Even in idyllic locations such as Indianapolis, Indiana, I was startled to learn that middle-class kids claimed to carry guns. Apparently, these fears are well founded, not like the monsters of childhood.

Consider the following statistics regarding willingness to carry a gun:

Teens Who Agree They Would Carry or Have Carried a Gun (Global Average 16 Percent)

Country	Percentage	Country	Percentage
Eastern Europe	25	India	18
United States	22	Western Europe	16
Latin America	21	Asia Pacific	7
Middle East	19	China	5

Knowing what concerns youth can provide rich material for poignancy in telling marketing stories. It is important to keep in mind, however, that the levels of intensity vary from country to country.

Some teens possess a strong feeling about the planet Earth and what will happen to it. These altruistic teenagers evince great concern for environmental issues and world peace. They are connected via organizations and the Internet to similar-minded teens in other countries.

It is CNN's ubiquitous, 24-hour global English broadcasting that brings the daily events of the world into the households where teenagers live. Since the U.S. superpower ranks as the most important country to these teens other than their own, the United States' global concerns become their own.

Marketers must grasp that although some teen worries are universal, other worries are specifically local. The smart multinational company recognizes both.

Differentiator 3: Love and Sex

Global teens may all be manufacturing hormones at the same rate, but the outlets and expectations for romantic interaction differ markedly by country and area.

Teen attitudes toward love and dating are segmented into three geographical areas: the liberal-minded attitude of the United States and Europe, the less liberal and more traditionally Catholic attitude of Latin America, and the strict traditional morality of most countries throughout Asia.

The importance to marketers is that knowing the differences in these three disparate areas will affect the product lines they offer, the packaging, and, most important, the advertising message.

The average incidence of dating among global teens is 36 percent. That's only 1 out of 3 teens around the globe going out on a date. When U.S. marketers see this statistic, it's just another example of local realities contradicting a general assumption.

The country with the highest rate of dating is Ukraine, at 67 percent. I wish I could tell you exactly why. One explanation is that Ukrainians marry young, so dating begins early.

Conversely, the lowest-ranking country for dating is Vietnam, at 12 percent. It's still a slower-developing nation tied to old-fashioned mores.

Teens—regardless of whether they date—undergo similar emotions and desires. These first youthful stirrings are universal; it is the acting out of these feelings that makes teens different in Chicago, Caracas, and Calcutta. In Paris, perhaps the romance capital of the world, it is not unusual to see young people holding hands, looking deeply into each other's eyes, and kissing on the street—whereas in Shanghai, the most prevalent public affection I've seen is between filial relations, such as grandparents and grandchildren.

During these teenage years, teens seek a validation of their worthiness through relationships. It represents the preliminary step on the road to coupling and marriage. They may travel collectively in packs, but even within the group there is much flirting and horseplay.

Western cultures offer teens opportunities for dating, which some Asian societies do not. Of the top 15 countries for teen dating, 12 are North American or European, including, Turkey, while 3 are South American (Brazil, Chile, and Venezuela). However, 9 of the bottom 10 countries for teen dating are Asian, with Nigeria the exception.

In essence, Asian teens are reserved, without the habit of openly expressed affection. This is evident by the "where they are at night" measure: Asian teens are home. Similarly, the stricter countries of Latin America also keep their children—especially their daughters—home in the evening.

It is in the area of love and sex, I suspect, that most advertisers make mistakes in developing global advertising to teens. Ads that are too overtly sexual, or show the female as the aggressor, are bound to be offensive or just plain weird to teens and parents in many parts

of the world. The repercussions could easily create a negative attitude toward a brand image that is only trying to be hip and relevant.

Differentiator 4: Drugs and Drinking

The facts are that drugs and drinking rank as the lowest of global
teen worries. I suspect that teens believe that alcohol and drugs are
always within their control. Marketers might imagine that teens
worldwide are binge drinkers, similar to many American college
students, but this not the case. Global teens are generally sober
and upright. If anything, they are buzzed by their caffeine and
sugar intake.

Cultural mores and tradition play a part in controlling the
drinking of teens. In Europe, teens are practically weaned on wine
and beer, so they do not have to face the coming-of-age drinking
reactions that exist in the United States. In addition, the easy
access in Europe to low-alcohol-content wine and beer reduces
the amount of drunkenness that comes from high-alcohol-content
hard liquor. Finally, in Asia, teens do not generally drink alcohol
unless it is served at home.

Teen drug use is also low worldwide. Although drugs, particularly marijuana, are available in the United States and in some
Western European and Latin American countries, illegal sub-
stances for teenagers are unheard of in Asia. Perhaps it is partly an
issue of permissiveness, and partly an issue of discretionary income.

Differentiator 5: Technological Access

Technology is not a level playing field. Technological access varies
sharply among global teens—although most teens have access to
television and radio, there is a marked difference in the degree of
computer literacy and in Internet usage.

Technological access varies among global teens.

Globally, the most significant finding is that an average of 81 percent of teens use a computer. (It should be noted, however, that these data are based on urban students in middle-class schools in major global markets.) Thirty of the forty-four countries in the study are at this 81 percent level or higher. What comes as a surprise is that the nation with the highest level of urban computer use is Peru, at over 90 percent, and an even greater shock is that Japan is the lowest, at 43 percent—19 percent lower than India, which is next to last at 64 percent.

The reasons for these totals will shed some light on the cultural differentiation between these countries. Peru welcomes the new technology and has installed computers in many schoolrooms, allowing its youth to begin learning skills early. Japan seeks to retain its centuries-old traditional methods of teaching and views the computer as an alien interloper into its historic system. Japan offers computer translators largely to college students. (As an aside, software translation into Japanese represents an ancillary problem.)

Internet usage measured in the New World Teen Study is a low 10 percent of global teens, with Sweden leading with 26 percent and the United States second with 24 percent. Many countries have low Internet access rates because of higher telephone costs with state monopolies. Getting online can be a complicated problem in places like Brazil and Beijing, where first getting a telephone is so difficult.

The French and Germans feel maligned because the official language of the Internet is English. The Internet demands a conversational ability in English, or nothing can be mastered online.

Differentiator 6: Responsibilities and Pressures

While teens the world over are expected to get good grades, there are many distinctions by country with respect to additional responsibilities. In many countries, young females are treated as second-class citizens. Teenage girls share similar tasks and assignments around the home. They help their mothers with housework, meal preparation, and, most important, taking care of younger siblings. These chores are not voluntary but mandatory, part of the traditional cultural heritage of many Asian and Latin American countries.

In addition, teenage girls in these societies are given the message that making a happy marriage and having a family will measure their success. However, this marriage-directed message is starting to conflict with the fact that young women in developing nations want to have careers.

When I was in Lima, Peru, a girl approached me at a youth workshop and told me she would so like to move to America. When I asked why, she said so that she could find an American husband who would let her have a career *and* children. "Latin men do not understand," she said, with genuine sadness in her eyes.

In Asian households, male and female teens are home doing schoolwork because the only path to success is via getting good grades and advancing to college. The economic note trumpeted to teens from these societies is to work hard now and play later when you have reached adulthood.

In the United States, a vastly different cultural and economic pattern exists for teens. With more than 50 percent working after school, American teens take steps to adulthood and fully mature consumerism earlier than their global counterparts.

The typical U.S. teen is juggling school, sports, work, family, and a social life at the same time. As consumers with discretionary income of their own, they learn how to make adult purchasing decisions in regard to sales and deals.

In Europe, the prevailing attitude remains that you are only young once, and this is the time to enjoy youth. A lower percentage of teens work, and thus most are still tied to their parents for an allowance. European teens enjoy out-of-house freedom, especially in urban areas, similar to what American youth also enjoys.

Although job one in Asia is to study hard, the roads to success diverge in Japan and China. Japan continues to emphasize the Old World sense of how to get ahead, relying on traditional methods of education and narrow career focus. China, emerging from a deep economic sleep, welcomes the new and encourages innovation.

Sadly, one of the major implications in all this is limited freedom in gender roles. When global advertising is developed for the youth target, marketers need to be sensitive to what is realistic as well as aspirational for each country.

Differentiator 7: Local Pride

I cannot emphasize enough how important it is to understand teens' local customs. It is also crucially important to comprehend the local meanings and symbolism of foreign icons in translation.

Faux Pas

An example of a cultural faux pas occurred when the National Basketball Association (NBA) promoted clothing for the Charlotte Hornets in South Korea. What the NBA did not realize was that wearing a green hat in Korea is a symbol of a cuckolded husband. Not surprisingly, sales did not meet expectations.

Marketers must be aware of special and diverse national histories and, most important, be sensitive to each particular nation's institutions, heroes, and cultural past. Individual countries' traditions offer companies an opportunity for success in promoting to teens on a local level.

Teens like to be recognized for achievements, whether these occur individually, at their school, or in their town. The local level—the lower level of the dual cultural passports route—provides marketers ingenious opportunities to salute teens where they live and where they play.

The opportunity is to make projects and promotions that are local work globally, and make global ones meaningful on a national or regional basis. Local advertising agencies are vital sources of information for what will work in a country and what will not. Indigenous journalists and educators are also excellent sources of often *free* information.

Local Pride

The Coca-Cola Company has one of the most sophisticated trends operations in the world, spearheaded by John Duke. John has put together an online network of experts in scores of countries who can answer questions about local culture in real time.

Faith Popcorn, a prominent futurist and founder of Brain Reserve, has a similar type of network for the United States. The point is that this kind of information is available cost-effectively for those marketers who are willing to search.

An excellent promotional example of establishing pride with a local outreach program is McDonald's All-American High School

Basketball Team, featuring the best high school players in the country. The team recognizes individual achievement and rewards the best players in the land. For McDonald's, the cost to recruit and maintain the All-American High School Basketball Team is worth the brand image and promotional benefits.

Any company's approach can be to tap into local events with a plan that earns the company recognition.

Differentiator 8: Values

Values are the ultimate differentiator among global teens. While some critical values are shared, as discussed in Chapter 3, there are many that focus the target into distinct segments of orientation around the world.

Values are formulated early and carried through a lifetime. They are shaped by a combination of parental influence, individual experience, local cultural realities, religion, and exposure to the world at large. Two kids on the same block in Park Forest, Illinois, where I grew up, might have very different values—just as you might vary radically from your next-door neighbor.

Values determine how teens will spend their money and their time. If you are a teen, it makes all the difference between having a tattoo and a belly ring and looking ready for a job on Wall Street. And that is just the outer manifestation.

The questions about values center on the main query of what drives teens. What determines their behavior? What are the influences on how and where they spend their money? What steps do they take to identify themselves? What do teens buy? What do they covet? Understanding the basis of their values will provide companies with the all-important key to unlock the global teen consumer potential. In the next chapter, the six behavioral segments of teenage values are discussed in detail. This segmentation is important for marketers because it indicates both in type and in numbers the real structure of global teenage culture.

No matter where teens live, the New World Teen Study segmentation based on values provides a simple framework for classification and understanding. Moreover, the incidence of values clusters shows strong geographic patterning. Equipped with this understanding, marketers can view a map of the world with an in-depth understanding of where their most likely targets reside.

5

The Six Values Segments of Global Youth: The Ultimate Differentiator

One of the most intriguing findings from the New World Teen Study is the existence of six distinct value segments for global youth. These segments define every aspect in a teen's life, from lifestyles to brand preferences. Understanding and leveraging these values segments will assist marketers in targeting and market sizing.

One of the most important facts to remember is that marketers cannot assume teens are alike worldwide except for the common cultural unifiers. Moreover, within a specific country, teens are not homogeneous. Within countries, their preferences depend largely on their classification within the six value segments.

An interesting exercise for executives in multinational companies is to sit on subways, trains, or buses in different countries and consider the diversity of the many types of teenagers. Don't just notice the kids with green spiked hair and pierced tongues. Look a little closer at the well-groomed kids with innocent, idyllic faces in school blazers or the teens that look identical to their parents except for their age. But I don't stop there. I have discovered first-hand that looks are also deceiving. It's what's inside the head and heart of teenagers that drives their behavior.

This segmentation analysis of values will prove useful to marketers because it determines who teens are, where teens live, and how many teens there are within countries. This knowledge has led global marketers such as Coca-Cola and Royal Philips Electronics to develop *common drivers* for ads and promotions that cut across national boundaries.

Values are the constructs on which teen behavior rests. It is important to note that values are established during the formative teen years and may not alter appreciably over a lifetime. A marketer who can recognize a teen target's value segment early on will have a good chance of keeping that teen as a valuable consumer for life.

Meet the Six Teen Segments

The New World Teen Study segmentation is based on what high school students around the world rate as the driving principles (values) that are important to them in life. It includes diverse values such as the following:

- *Relationship with family*
- *Accomplishing as much as possible*
- *Having as much fun as possible*
- *Relationships with friends*
- *Making the world a better place*
- *Being accepted as an individual*
- *Upholding time-honored customs, traditions, and values*
- *Never being bored*

The values themselves were derived from the academic work of leading theorists Dr. Sholom Schwartz and Dr. Milton Rokeasch. Both were pioneers in the area of international values. At Brain-

ves we consulted with Dr. Schwartz, modified his work to
t input from our own earlier research with teens, and adapted
lues to develop a battery of questions for classification.

results reveal a clearly segmented teen society based on
values that are significant to individual teens. Segment clas-
on reveals what drives teens, what they care about, what
hem up at night, and what kind of future they envision for
themselves. It also determines how they will spend their money,
what products they want most, how advertising will grab them,
and what brands will succeed in reaching their hearts.

In essence, a marketer can plot the following segments along a
value wheel of teen orientation based on the illustration of being
inner directed (me) versus outer directed (we), conformist or non-
conformist.

The New World Teen Study uncovered six distinct and disparate value clusters of teen behavior. Teens can be defined in the
following groups:

The values wheel.

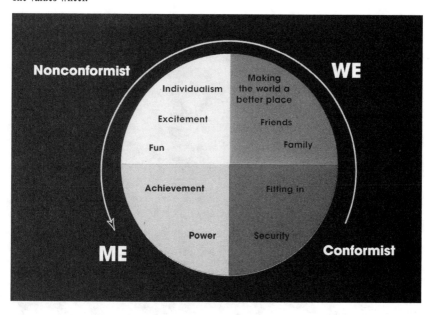

Segments	Percentage Worldwide*
Thrills and chills	18
Upholders	16
Quiet achievers	15
Resigned	14
Bootstrappers	14
World savers	12

The segmentation values act as behavioral filters that determine how teens make their way in the world. This analysis sheds light on why teens in Amsterdam pierce body parts, why youth in Brazil are worried about AIDS, why Japanese youth are approaching the edge of rebellion, and why U.S. teens seem so motivated to achieve. In part, it can be a funciton of whether teens are home or inner directed, conformists or nonconformists.

*Numbers total 89 percent, with 11 percent nonclassified.

Teen orientation grid.

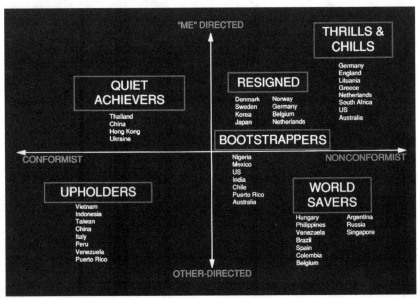

New World Teen Study values cluster breakdown.

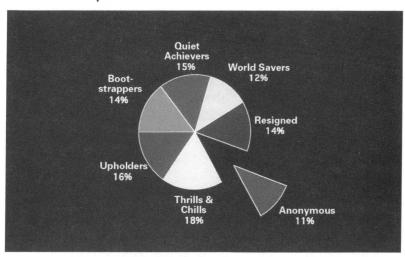

Segment 1: Thrills and Chills (18 Percent)

Key countries (incidence above global average): Germany, England
Lithuania, Greece, Netherlands, South Africa, United State

> Belgium, Canada, Turkey, France, Poland, Japan, Italy, Denmark, Argentina, and Norway
> *Key definers:* Fun, friends, irreverence, and sensation

The Who, What, and Where

The thrills-and-chills teens reflect what it is like to be young, somewhat of a stereotype of the devil-may-care, trying-to-become-independent hedonist. For the most part, they come from affluent or middle-class parents, live mainly in developed countries, and have allowance money to spend. These teens manifest a conspicuous sensualism and seek to push the pedal on life's enjoyments to the max.

Marketers should realize that this group always has its collective antennae out, seeking to use or to consume the novel and the new. It is no surprise that this segment represents the largest base of teen consumers.

These kids love to buy stuff, and they do not mind paying the price for expensive items. The prevalent attitude is that "I'm only young once, and I want to enjoy it whatever the cost."

These teens reside mostly in Europe where they have easy entry to being out at night. They love to dine at restaurants with friends, meet at a pub or a café, and go dating or dancing. These are the smokers and drinkers you see throughout Europe who emulate the adult behavior of their parents.

Music is central to the collective weltanschauung; they love to attend concerts and to buy the newest CDs. Rock stars and rock bands around the world are their heroes, and they are keen to find the latest new group or hip soloist. In addition, they are ardent MTV watchers and are interested in the new digital television (DTV) technology.

Marketing Approach

Thrills-and-chills teens respond to sensory stimulation. They tend to get bored easily, so stale advertising messages will escape their notice. They want action ads with bells and whistles, humor, novelty, color, and sound.

Thrills-and-Chills Teens' Driving Principles: Fun, Excitement, and Friends

Enjoy	Worry About	Attitudes	Own/Wear/Do
■ Going out to eat (+) ■ Going to a bar (+) ■ Drinking wine/beer (+) ■ Smoking cigarettes (+) ■ Going to a party (+) ■ Going on a date (+) ■ Going dancing (+)	■ Finding someone to love (+) ■ An unplanned pregnancy (+) ■ Not looking good enough (+)	■ I am in love (+) ■ I would dye or have dyed my hair (+) ■ I would like to have a tattoo or nose/lip/belly ring (+)	■ Fast food (+) ■ Acne medication (+) ■ Perfume/cologne (+) ■ Deodorant/ antiperspirant (+) ■ Have a job to earn money (–) ■ Attend religious services (–)

Note: Plus signs mean higher than global average; minus signs mean lower than global average.

These kids are edgier than their peers are, and they constantly seek out the new. They are the first ones on the block to hear of the newest technology, the hippest Web site, and the latest form of excitement.

Experimenting is second nature. They sport all sorts of body rings and wear their hair in different shades. (Bright primary colors of red, blue, and yellow are hot right now in Melbourne.) They may be acquainted with drugs, particularly marijuana. They probably have sexual experiences earlier than the other five groups. Not surprisingly, unplanned pregnancy ranks as one of their prime worries.

In essence, these are the popular kids in high school, the trendsetters, who exhibit the élan that the other kids try to copy. This group possesses style and personality—a little like the first hippies of the 1960s. Thrills-and-chills teens are cool.

Summary

Thrills-and-chills teens expect everything in life and make it a goal to get as much of the good times as they can. They have ample money and like to spend it, which makes them the foremost group for marketers to consider. Spending and shopping are normal activities, and they develop loyalties to those brands that speak their language. Their motto is "Let the good times roll," and for thrills-and-chills teens, they do.

Segment 2: Resigned (14 Percent)

> *Key countries:* Denmark, Sweden, Korea, Japan, Norway, Germany, Belgium, Netherlands, Argentina, Canada, Turkey, England, Spain, France, and Taiwan
> *Key definers:* Friends, fun, family, and *low* expectations

The Who, What, and Where

The resigned have very low expectations for their futures. At an early age, they perceive that their lot in the world has already been

determined. They exhibit an inescapable fatalism from which they perceive there is no exit. The success train has pulled out of the station, and they are not on it.

The resigned resemble the thrills-and-chills teens, often decorating their bodies with rings and dye. However, the resigned are alienated from society and very pessimistic about their chances for economic success.

Teens in this group tend to see the dark side—they are the punk rockers of the world, who sometimes take drugs and drink to excess. They may act out negative and destructive behavior arising from frustration and envy. In Western Europe, these can be the soccer thugs who travel in packs on Saturday game days looking for a punch up.

The resigned in Europe often come from blue-collar homes, with parents who are factory workers or clerks. The dreary despair of the parents' lower-income lives filters down to the children. These teens feel trapped in repeating the cheerless lives of their elders, without hope for a better future.

They also come from countries with strong welfare mentalities. One of their greatest worries is the potential loss of social programs, the safety net that socialism offers. In Japan and Korea, the hive and worker-bee mentality demands strict discipline.

The resigned respond to heavy metal and grunge music that emphasizes the negative and angry side of society. They endorse the message that the world is a rough-and-tumble place that does not offer much comfort.

Finally, the resigned do not participate in many activities outside of school. They score low on going to the movies, attending cultural events such as plays or the opera, or even visiting relatives. For the resigned, the world is gray, and boredom is a major factor.

Marketing Approach

The resigned do not have as much discretionary income to spend as teens in other segments. They do not consume many high-ticket products and score low on all indexes of owning electronic or technological products. They tend to be infrequent consumers save for some fast food, low-ticket clothes items, tobacco, and alcohol.

Further, the resigned do respond to certain kinds of advertising and promotional messages. They are drawn to irony and to ads that make fun of the pompousness of society. Naturally, they tend to be cynical about overly happy communications that portray an optimistic world.

Summary

It would be easy for companies to write off the resigned as being a weak target market for goods and services. However, there are huge numbers of teens in this group who have some income to spend, and they emulate the thrills-and-chills crowd. Consequently, it would be easy to target the resigned and thrills-and-chills teens with the same marketing efforts.

The Resigned's Driving Principles: Fun, Friends, and Low Expectations

ENJOY	WORRY ABOUT	ATTITUDES
■ Doing something artistic creative (–)	■ Getting a university degree (–)	■ I would dye or have dyed my hair (+)
■ Attending an opera, play or ballet (–)	■ Not being treated with respect (–)	■ I enjoy learning about new things (–)
■ Visiting relatives (–)	■ The economy (–)	■ I try to get access to new technology as soon as it is available (–)
	■ Not living up to others' expectations (–)	
	■ Destruction of rain forest (–)	
	■ Global warming (–)	

Note: Plus signs mean higher than global average; minus signs mean lower than global average.

Segment 3: World Savers (12 Percent)

Key countries: Hungary, Philippines, Venezuela, Brazil, Spain, Colombia, Belgium, Argentina, Russia, Singapore, France, Poland, Ukraine, Italy, South Africa, Mexico, and England
Key definers: Environment, humanism, fun, and friends

The Who, What, and Where
The world savers (aka café altruists) are the models of what gives hope to the next generation. These are the "good kids," the responsible ones possessed of a world soul. These teens care—they *really* care.

Altruism is the most significant attribute of this value segment. These teens have a long list of do-good global and local causes that spark their interest and their participation. Whether the goal is to combat racism, save the rain forest, or curtail global warming, the world savers are marching at the forefront, trying to effect some positive change

These teens are the intelligentsia in most countries who do well in school. They are the class and club leaders who join many organizations. Grades and higher education are important, not only to succeed in finding a better paying job but, more important, to provide careers in which they can practice their altruism—they aspire to be doctors, nurses, forest rangers, social workers, and environmentalists.

World savers attend the same parties as the thrills-and-chills kids. However, they are not motivated by the new and exciting. These teens are more into romance, relationships, and strong friendships, and they have a wonderful feeling for meeting people.

This segment soaks up culture, some of it surprisingly highbrow. These teens eagerly attend concerts, operas, and plays. They exhibit a joie de vivre about life and enjoy dancing or drinking at bars and cafés with friends. They love the outdoors as well, including, camping, hiking, and other sports activities. However, they are not the school jocks.

The world savers are prevalent in many Latin American countries where their Catholicism is blended with humanism. Moreover, this segment is also well represented in Hungary and Russia, former Eastern Bloc countries seeking new definition and respect. The teens in these two countries do not want a return to Cold War politics.

Marketing Approach

World savers will be attracted by honest and sincere messages that tell the truth. They are offended by any ad that puts people down or makes fun of another group. They are sophisticated enough to have a sense of humor; they just do not want to laugh at anyone's foibles.

It is important to note that a marketer can piggyback a promotion with a worthwhile cause, and have world savers respond positively to that message.

World Savers' Driving Principles: Achievement and Conformity

Enjoy	Worry About	Attitudes	Own/Wear/Do
■ Attending an opera, play, or ballet (+)	■ Racism (+)	■ I am in love (+)	■ Deodorant/ antiperspirant (+)
■ Doing something artistic or creative (+)	■ Poverty for others (+)	■ I would carry or have carried a gun (−)	
■ Taking photos (+)	■ The environment (+)		
■ Going camping or hiking (+)	■ AIDS (+)		
■ Going to a bar (+)	■ Being at war (+)		
■ Going dancing (+)	■ Terrorism (+)		
	■ Being able to have children (+)		
	■ Finding someone to love (+)		

Note: Plus signs mean higher than global average; minus signs mean lower than global average.

Summary
World savers are smart and avid consumers. They are technologically advanced and understand e-commerce and computers. In sum, these kids seek value and importance for what they buy.

Segment 4: Quiet Achievers (15 Percent)

Key countries: Thailand, China, Hong Kong, Ukraine, Korea, Lithuania, Russia, and Peru

Key definers: Success, anonymity, anti-individualism, and social optimism

The Who, What, and Where

Quiet achievers value anonymity and prefer to rest in the shadows. These teens are the least rebellious of all the groups, conforming to the mores of local society. They do not make waves, avoid the limelight, and do not ever want to stand out in the crowd. These are the bookish and straight kids who study long hours.

One important trait is their fierce ambition. They are highly goal directed. Their top priority is to make good grades in school and use higher education to further their career advancement. The drive for success stems from parents who are eager for their children to do well. The parents instill in their children the importance of discipline and the value of homework.

Quiet achievers have strong family ties and realize that success reflects back upon the family. Their main worry is not living up to parental expectations. A teen who acts out in school or is disrespectful can bring disgrace upon the family.

Most of the quiet achievers live in Asia, especially Thailand and China. But these somewhat stereotypical studious types also exist in the United States, where they are sometimes regarded as being techies or nerds. Worldwide, the common thread among

quiet achievers is their drive to accomplish something without making waves or attracting too much attention.

These teens are rarely out in the evening unless it is to study with friends. They avoid going to parties or drinking.

Marketing Approach
Quiet achievers are prime consumers who love to purchase stuff. Although they may appear to recede into the background, they emerge into the daylight of shopping. Part of the reward for working diligently is being able to buy products.

The parents of quiet achievers often have some wealth, sometimes even large sums of money. They have the financial ability to give children allowances. Moreover, the parents will defer to their children's needs when it comes to computers and other technological products that will aid in homework.

This group is also keen on music, and these teens will spend money on CDs and stereo equipment. They are inner directed and adept at creating their own good times. International marketers

Quiet Achievers' Driving Principles: Achievement and Conformity

Enjoy	Worry About	Attitudes	Own/Wear/Do
■ Studying (+)	■ Not living up to others' expectations (+)	■ The world will improve in my lifetime (+)	■ Have a job to earn money (–)
■ Listening to music (+)	■ Finishing my education (–)	■ The education I am getting is good preparation for the future (–)	■ Backpack (–)
■ Visiting museums (+)	■ An unplanned pregnancy (–)		■ Blue jeans (–)
■ Going to parties (–)	■ Taking drugs (–)	■ Somehow or other I will have a good life (–)	■ Athletic shoes (–)
■ Drinking wine/beer (–)	■ Smoking too much (–)	■ I would dye or have dyed my hair	*Girls*
	■ AIDS (–)	■ I would like to have a tattoo or nose/lip/belly ring (+)	■ Lipstick (–)
			■ Nail polish (–)
			■ Mascara (–)

Note: Plus signs mean higher than global average; minus signs mean lower than global average.

who have seized upon the music angle as a promotional niche can easily reach these teens. Others can find them through television.

Quiet achievers are serious minded and prefer ads that address the benefits of a product. They are embarrassed by ads that display rampant sexuality. And they do not respond to the sarcastic or the irreverent.

Summary

The quiet achievers go through their teen years with determination and restraint. They have a singular purpose—to study hard and do well in school. Their preoccupation with scholastic accomplishment limits their enjoyment of other teen activities.

Segment 5: Bootstrappers (14 Percent)

> Key countries: Nigeria, Mexico, United States, India, Chile, Puerto Rico, Peru, Venezuela, Colombia, and South Africa
> Key definers: Achievement, individualism, optimism, determination, and power

The Who, What, and Where

The bootstrappers are perhaps the most intriguing of the six groups because of their enthusiastic determination to succeed. These are the kids who make their parents proud, or at least try hard to please. They are the starry-eyed optimists who cannot wait for adulthood to take the world for all it has to offer. They exude an unrestrained joy about teen life, stating, "Hello, world, here I am."

These teens spend a lot of time at home, doing homework and helping around the house. They are highly family oriented and seek out parents for advice and support. In addition, they enjoy spending time with relatives and going to church. Nevertheless, they manifest a healthy separation from the family as they pursue many independent activities.

Their key goal is achievement, but this aim is not exclusively scholastic. The bootstrappers are eager for power; they are the politicians in every high school who covet the class offices. They view the use of authority as a means for securing rewards, and they are constantly seeking out recognition.

Geographically, many of these teens come from emerging nations such as Nigeria and India. These teens have hopes and dreams that the world will improve in their lifetime. They also believe that they will contribute to its betterment.

In the United States, bootstrappers represent 1 in every 4 teens. Moreover, they represent 40 percent of young African-Americans. A major error of U.S. marketers is to misread the size and purchasing power of this ambitious African-American segment. Misconceptions concerning ethnic youth in the United States have caused some marketers to misunderstand and forget to target this segment for technology and high-ticket items. In sum, a majority of African-American teens are serious minded, wanting to make success happen and, increasingly, they are finding the answer through higher education and achievement.

Finally, even though bootstrappers want access to power, they are not willing to pursue achievement at a destructive cost. They are well behaved, respectful, and have little if any desire to rebel against society. If anything, bootstrappers want to play by society's rules to succeed.

Marketing Approach

Bootstrappers are young yuppies in training. They want the best life has to offer, and that means premium brands and luxury goods. Emphasizing quality, status, and performance in a product is certain to catch a bootstrapper's eye. More so than any other segment (almost tied with the thrills-and-chills teens), Bootstrappers are likely to say, "When I really want a brand, price doesn't matter."

Bootstrappers are also on the lookout for goods and services that will help them get ahead. They want to dress for success, have access to technology and software, and stay plugged into the world of media and culture for insights that will give them a competitive edge.

Because bootstrappers have an optimistic view of their own world, they are attracted by messages that portray aspirations and possibilities for products and their users.

Summary

Bootstrappers are today's teen achievers and tomorrow's leaders. They are determined to succeed financially and do not necessarily want to wait to enjoy the pleasures of conspicuous consumption. Brands that convincingly connect to the positive values of the good life will stand a strong chance with these teens. Moreover, marketers who can connect with this segment stand the chance for a long run of repeat purchases.

Bootstrappers' Driving Principles: Achievement, Determination, and Individualism

ENJOY	WORRY ABOUT	ATTITUDES	OWN/WEAR/DO
■ Spending time with family (+) ■ Visiting relatives (+)	■ Not having friends (−) ■ Being lonely (−)	■ The education I am getting is good preparation for the future (+) ■ Somehow or other I know I will have a good life (+) ■ The world will improve in my lifetime (+)	■ Attend religious services (+) ■ Receive an allowance (−)

Note: Plus signs mean higher than global average; minus signs mean lower than global average.

Segment 6: Upholders (16 Percent)

Key countries: Vietnam, Indonesia, Taiwan, China, Italy, Peru,
Venezuela, Puerto Rico, India, Philippines, and Singapore
Key definers: Family, custom, tradition, and respect for individuals

The Who, What, and Where

The upholders are the most dreamy and childlike of the six segments. They retain many attributes of adolescence, appearing seemingly slow to make a leap into adulthood. In essence, they live sheltered and ordered lives that seem bereft of many forms of typical teen fun and wild adult-emulating teen behavior.

These teens behave dutifully and adhere to the strictly held beliefs of their families and countries. They conform to the norms of societal standards, willing to march in the same line and in the same attire as their peers. Traditions act as a rigid guideline, and these teens would be hard pressed to rebel or confront authority.

Upholders are different from quiet achievers in that they do not have overwhelming ambitions to succeed. They are content to rest comfortably in the mainstream of life, remaining unnoticed.

The girls seek mostly to get married and have families; they have little desire for a career. The boys perceive that they are fated to have jobs similar to their fathers' or at least close to what the family expects. Many of these teens will make up the middle-class fabric of their countries, with jobs ranging from blue-collar, trades, and civil service positions.

Upholders predominate in Asian countries, such as Indonesia and Vietnam, that value old traditions and extended family relationships. Teens in these countries are helpful around the home and protective of their siblings.

Moreover, many upholders are in Catholic countries where the Church and tradition guide schooling, attitudes, and values.

Upholders do not want to set the world on fire, nor are they into controversy. They are inner directed, although they do have a heart for helping to create a better world even if they do not plan to see much of it firsthand. Enjoying a rewarding family life and fitting into society measure their success.

Marketing Approach

Advertisers and marketers have had success selling to upholders using youthful, almost childlike communication and fun messages. These are teens who still watch cartoons and are avid media consumers. They are highly involved in both watching and playing sports, particularly basketball and soccer. More than any other group, they plan to live in their country of birth throughout adulthood. Therefore, the local route of the dual cultural passport is highly meaningful to them.

Essentially, upholders are homebodies. They are deeply rooted in family and community, like to make purchase decisions that are safe, and conform to their parents' values. Brands that take a leadership stance will attract upholders for their risk-free quality, value, and reliability.

Upholders' Driving Principles: Family and Tradition

ENJOY	WORRY ABOUT	ATTITUDES	OWN/WEAR/DO
■ Reading books (+) ■ Spending time with family (+) ■ Visiting relatives (+)	■ Not living up to others' expectations (+)	■ The world will improve in my lifetime (+) ■ I would like to wear a tattoo or nose/lip/belly ring (–) ■ I would carry or have carried a gun (–)	■ Have a job to earn money (–) ■ Fast food (–) ■ Deodorant/antiperspirant (–) Girls ■ Lipstick (–) ■ Mascara (–) ■ Nail polish (–)

Note: Plus signs mean higher than global average; minus signs mean lower than global average.

Summary

Upholders are the quiet good teen citizens of the world. They plan to follow in their parents' footsteps and hope to live up to their families' expectations. Upholders do not like to take consumer risks and are attracted to brands with proven track records and authenticity. Once won over, however, they are highly likely to be loyal for a lifetime, given their comfort with the familiar and their reticence toward change.

Conclusion

While each of these segments is distinct in personality and internal drives, there are many commonalities that make targeting more than one segment at a time an achievable reality. If your product is about fashion and fun or being on the cutting edge, then the thrills-and-chills and resigned teens, and the world savers are likely to respond to a common message. If your pitch is about getting ahead, then the quiet achievers, bootstrappers, and world savers will be all ears.

In a later chapter I will show you how to examine these segments in light of their prevalent geography, to develop target messages that will succeed internationally. But first, let's take an in-depth look through the regional lens of influences detailed in Chapter 6.

6

Regional Broad Strokes

When an advertising strategist sits down to develop a global teen advertising strategy, it is too cumbersome to begin looking at youth culture on a country-by-country basis. Instead, there is a need for *regional broad strokes* that help put the regional teen cultural differences in perspective. In this chapter, I try to paint a macroview of what a marketer should keep in mind when thinking about regional differences. Granted, it is only one lens by which to examine the marketplace, and many should be used. However, it is a very practical starting point, as I know from experience.

Savvy marketers need to understand how regions are generally different from the rest of the world, while at the same time understanding how individual countries within a region vary, often radically. In this book there are several tables that show incidence levels for all types of attitudes and behaviors on a country-by-country basis. Look at any table, and note that in most cases a region will have representative countries in the high, middle, and low ranges of the spectrum. While each country's culture should be reviewed as a filter against any marketing communications plan to ensure a proper fit, there are some useful regional perspectives that can be referred to as rules of thumb.

The United States: Center of Global Teen Culture

The United States is so important as the capital of the new world teen culture that I treat it as both a country and a region. The concept of what constitutes a global teenage life today is the evolving product of 60 years of American culture. From the bobby-soxers of the 1940s, to the new-car culture of suburbia in the 1950s, the longhaired hippies of the 1960s, the disco dancers of the 1970s, and, finally, the jeans-wearing mall kids of the 1990s, the cliché of what is unusual and exciting about teen life is the American teenager.

The world has tried to copy the U.S. jeans, sneakers, and backpack look. Over time, American teens have set the standards for the different cultural variables that make being a teen cool. But remember that the United States as fount and source of teen behavior exists both in domestic reality and as a foreign lifestyle fantasy.

Conspicuous consumerism is one of the main reasons why global teens try to emulate Americans. Our movies and television programs have created images of U.S. teens who seem to have unlimited cash to spend in malls, shops, and restaurants on a daily basis. Nothing seems beyond the reach of these American teenagers. In this modern fairy tale, clothing is in infinite variety, musical equipment and CDs abound, and, of course, there is a huge mound of fast food all around.

The clear message is that American teens exist to please themselves by being perpetual shoppers. The underscored message to youth in other countries, regardless of whether it is intentional, is that maybe you can sample some part of this U.S. experience.

The overriding communiqué is that American teens never have to wait to gratify their appetites. U.S. youth demonstrates the practiced experience of how to buy stuff.

In reality, more than 50 percent of U.S. teens work, and this explains in part why they have such massive purchasing power. By working many hours during the week, these teens tend to have the same job worries as their parents. They lead miniadult job lives with deadlines, long hours, and a paycheck.

Owing to the many activities of work and school, marketers have a difficult time reaching U.S. teens. American teens do not have much time to sit around and watch television or read newspapers or magazines. U.S. youth represents a moving target that must be reached in innovative ways—which explains why marketers are enamored with advertising on the Internet and other interactive media.

The booming U.S. economy continues to employ millions of teens. Any teen in the city or the suburbs can find part-time work and earn money. Teens in the United States spend $27 billion annually, with probably as much as 50 percent coming from their own employment.

Independence for U.S. teens comes from earning pocket money and not being tied to parental purse strings. This current self-sufficiency is markedly a U.S. phenomenon, because other nations do not offer similar employment opportunities to youth.

As the archetype for teenage behavior globally, the United States is regarded as the capital of teen culture. What plays in Santa Monica or Westport will likely play in Nottingham or New Delhi because the United States symbolizes cool to teens right now.

Western Europe: Economic Alienation

Western European teens are sitting on the horns of a dilemma. Although, the European Union promises greater economic efficiency for its member states, at the same time it reconstructs or eliminates treasured national perquisites. The uncertainty of what will happen in this great economic and cultural shift has caused anxiety that is reflected in a pessimistic attitude among teens.

Economic experts anticipate a substantial change in the way Western Europe does business by the year 2010. The changeover from individual national currencies to the euro will be finalized in 2002, when the new money enters circulation as cash for consumer purchases in all member countries except the United Kingdom.

Nevertheless, European teens are not yet fully enjoying the promised boon of an amalgamated Europe. Today's teens are leery that traditional social benefits may not exist when they reach adulthood.

Western European teens are apprehensive that the cost of maintaining the welfare system and its benefits will increase significantly in the future. Without the guarantee of the safety net in the areas of employment, housing, and health care, teens in Europe remain uncertain as to their prospects.

This vagueness about the future has fostered some spirit of alienation and resignation. Some Western European teens act as though they cannot escape an impending cloud of doom. So many act out a devil-may-care, a let's-live-for-the-moment frenetic approach to life. They drink. They smoke. They are sexually active. They are out at night. Not all of them, of course, but a conspicuous segment of the thrills-and-chills and resigned teens. It is altogether a mixture of fatalism and hedonism.

Western European teens seek time to enjoy the pleasures of life. Free time is what these libertarians value most. It is the utilization of time that allows for individual statements.

Although Western European teens do not celebrate purchasing goods and having stuff to the extent of their American counterparts, they represent an interesting consumer market, especially the thrills-and-chills crowd that dominates the continent. These teens are open to a broad range of products and messages, with fun being the overriding aim. Basically, they are looking for ads that amuse and products that thrill.

European teens are more liberal in style and dress. They enjoy showing off their individualism by wearing bright colors and odd combinations of attire. For many, rings in the nose, the ear, and, occasionally, the belly button, are part of the style statement.

European teens are avid newspaper readers, partially because of the ongoing abundance of newspapers in their countries. While newspaper readership has seriously declined in the United States, this medium still plays a vital role in many European countries, providing a political slant.

A little-known but important fact is the importance of reaching these teens via outdoor marketing. This medium is powerful because Western European teens are out a lot, including nights and weekends. In addition, they are able to view billboards and signs painted on buildings as they ride on bikes, motor scooters, trains, and buses.

Eastern Europe: Hardened Realism after the Fall

The teens of Eastern Europe are being pulled in many different directions. They are both cynical and practical at the same time. The many years of life under communism has cast a film over their hopes and dreams. These teens are desperately searching for economic prosperity and a future brighter than the lives of past generations.

Eastern Europe cannot be fitted into a single observation that represents all countries. The measurement of a successful shift from communism to economic capitalism varies by how well each country is doing. Three tiers define the economic ranking of Eastern Europe:

1. Enjoying improved economic success: East Germany, Poland, and the Czech Republic
2. Enjoying some economic success: Russia, Hungary, Romania, Slovakia, and Ukraine
3. Still striving for a leg up economically: Bulgaria, Croatia, Albania, Latvia, Lithuania, Estonia, and the many other countries of the former Soviet Union

The Eastern European teen rides on a teeter-totter of fluctuating economic changes. Russia is a prime example. At one point in 1998, Russia seemed to be on the verge of an economic turnaround, and prosperity loomed around the corner. Then the economy collapsed, and the "miracle" bubble burst.

These teens look foremost to their neighbors in the West in order to copy the style of what it is like to be a European teen. Eastern European teens aspire to approach the levels of freedom and consumerism enjoyed by their European Union peers. This is visible in the streets of Prague, Budapest, and Warsaw, where, at first glance, teens seem no different in style and demeanor from teens in Paris, Brussels, or Madrid.

A good place to witness the yearning of these teens for that Western experience is at the Trieste, Italy, railroad station any week in July and August. Thousands of tourists, all from Eastern European countries, including many teenagers alone or with their families, pour into this ancient Adriatic port city on a direct railroad line from Moscow. When they embark, the smiles on their enthusiastic faces say, "I'm in the West, and it's fabulous."

Southeast Asia: Modern Traditionalism

The teens in Southeast Asia—the countries of Vietnam, Laos, Cambodia, Thailand, Philippines, and Korea—experience a polarization of emotion between wanting both to defer to centuries of tradition and yet savor a taste of the new. The crux of the problem is to remain distinctly Asian and, at the same time, embrace a Western concept of consumerism and modernity. Global marketers are faced with the dilemma of understanding whether a country is longing for the future or pining for the past.

The arrival of television to cities and even remote villages in Southeast Asia has depicted a world of Western styles and strange cultures. No longer can these countries remain isolated from the global brands whose advertising they see on local television. Now that these brands are found in stores, it's natural that Southeast Asians want to become consumers.

Teens in these countries are among the most status conscious in the world, mainly because status and pecking order in this area of the world have traditionally defined who a person is. Few global marketers have understood this centuries-old phenomenon, but it pervades all aspects of daily life. To paraphrase Descartes' statement about existence, "I buy status brands, therefore I am."

The striving to own the "best" brand pervades the culture and explains why heavily advertised and marketed brands predominate. Families do not buy just any television; they try to purchase the best model. Showing off to friends and neighbors becomes a form of conspicuous consumption. Sometimes, as I have previously mentioned observing in China, they will even leave the tags visible on high-ticket items, especially electronic products.

Southeast Asian teens have positive hopes for the future and are eager to ride on the coattails of their countries' attempts to industrialize. Over the past 20 years, career and job potentials for teens have improved with the shifting of ready-to-wear clothing manufacturing to this area. The low labor rates paid by many apparel companies have caused a righteous stir around the world, but to many Southeast Asians low wages are better than no wages.

An additional fact for marketers to know about Southeast Asia is the importance of parental assistance in helping children succeed. Southeast Asian parents are rooting their children on, confident that by a combination of education and access to the best technology, their children can find professional careers of high standing.

China: The New Capitalists

China is so vast that, like America, it is both a country and a region. Chinese teens strive to be the new capitalists of the world. No country now aspires more to grab the gold ring of prosperity than does China.

This is one of the significant reasons why global marketers are so enthused over the prospect of introducing and promoting brands and setting up distribution channels. China is eager to advance into the consumer future, and all multinational companies want to have operations in place when it does.

Foremost, the number of teens in China is enormous: 98 *million*. A large percentage of this teen population lives in or near the larger cities and marketing areas, so it is possible to reach large numbers with a major promotion or event.

Emerging into the sunlight of capitalism after having dwelt in the dark of a drab Maoist past, Chinese youth is eager to catch up with Western styles and consumer comforts. They are also eager to create their own sense of style. Items coming from the U.S. and Europe have the advantage of seeming cool. They include professional athletic jerseys, sneakers, cosmetics, and even fast food. Chinese teens are reaching for it all.

I have been told about a Chinese yuppie strategy emerging that helps fuel the desire for consumer goods. Often, aspiring young married couples will try to have one spouse work for a Chinese company while the other works for a Western one. The former receives state health and housing benefits, while the latter receives a higher salary, which provides substantially greater expendable income to the family. In other words, there is a strong motivation among Chinese youth and young adults to create an economic good life for themselves and their families.

South America: The Land of Soulful Dreamers

South American teens have a different worldview from other teens. Basically, they feel left out of the ongoing process of world progress. Too often, they perceive that their countries are mired in the old traditions, the old politics, and the old economics.

An additional problem is that centuries of worker exploitation have produced a two-caste system of haves and have-nots. The haves come from families with money and contacts and go to the best schools. The have-nots are rural and barrio kids whose families have dwelt in poverty for decades. However, in several countries there is an attempt to level the playing field with improved and universal education. Putting computers in the classroom as has been done in Lima, for instance, will allow for quick strides.

The thing to consider is the universal desire to develop and catch up with the world technologically and economically. Like Western Europeans, South Americans love their local culture. However, unlike Western Europeans, they seem to feel more confident about holding on to their culture amid rapid change.

When I think of South American teens I think of music and laughter—the sparkle in their eyes and their passion for living. There is a spirit among Latin youth that is uniquely human and optimistic. These teens embrace the world for all its joyousness and are delightfully open to the world at large. Marketing to youth in South America can be so effective when it shares in this celebration of life.

A Word of Caution

Probably the most common of the dangerous mistakes that global marketers make is assuming that regions can always be treated as a unified whole. Western marketers know, for instance, that Asia or South America are very different, but there is often little sense of the vast differences between cultures within the same region, sometimes even between countries that border one another.

If you remember one practical insight from this book that goes beyond a general understanding of today's global youth culture, it should be this: *Do not assume regional homogeneity!* Asia is perhaps the worst place to generalize about because it contains such distinct and diverse cultures. The Japanese teen market, for instance, is economically like that of the United States, operating in a spend, spend, spend mode, and culturally more like that of Western Europe, with a large percentage of the thrills-and-chills and resigned segments.

Compare this with the neighboring Chinese teen. The Chinese teen is in many ways culturally close to the U.S. teen, but radically different in consumer habits. Chinese teens are ambitious and optimistic about the future. The Japanese teens next door are worried and frustrated over rigid social rules. Will the same advertising work in both Japan and China? Possibly, if the marketers artfully work the generational unifiers. However, these market differences have to be understood and evaluated in the context of any planned marketing efforts to assure success within a region. It is more likely that a television campaign designed for Western Europe should run in Japan and advertising developed for the United States should run in China. It all depends on the message and tonality. But *effective marketers must learn to think outside of geographic boundaries and think in terms of targets by their values segments, aspirations, and outlooks.*

One strong illustration of this point is to consider critical attitudes in each country under consideration.

The table shows the levels of agreement with two revealing statements:

- I am in love.
- I try to get access to new electronics/technology as soon as I can.

Percent Agreement, Regional Diversity

Statement	United States	China	Vietnam	Japan
I am in love.	42	5	17	33
I try to get access to new electronics/technology as soon as I can.	33	46	50	15

Perhaps you did a double take at the level of interest Japanese teens have in accessing new technology. I did too, the first time I saw these levels. The fact is that Japanese teens live in a culture that is inundated with technology to the point that they almost take it for granted. Maybe it is a little like working in a candy factory and having your fill. At the same time, Japanese teens have not had the Internet opened to them in the classrooms because of resistance to computers among Japanese educators. I believe that once Japanese teens gain computer access, their attitudes toward technology will rapidly change.

A noteworthy finding is that countries from disparate continents can be more alike than their nearest neighbors. In the next chapter I examine these important differences among countries and implications for marketers.

7

Eighteen Country Snapshots

I want to provide you with a snapshot picture of teens in many locations of the world because it is important to see the individual differences that exist from one country to the next. The emphasis is on many of the countries that are members of the $1 Billion Club, meaning they have annual teen spending of at least $1 billion. However, there are some others, such as Ukraine, Hong Kong, Spain, and Turkey, that are included just because they are so interesting. Teen culture really comes alive when you zero in on it nation by nation and examine how different countries perceive the world. These data came from the New World Teen Study—Wave II.

The findings, as you will see, reinforce my earlier promise that marketers cannot generalize about teens. Second, neighboring countries are not all alike—borders have historically erected cultural and societal barriers.

What you should take away from this country-by-country analysis is a snapshot of the unique qualities and culture of teens in each nation. Perhaps you'll be surprised as I was by the distinct differences and by significant nuances.

I selected 18 nations to give a representative portrait of the regions of the world, choosing some of the countries that should be of greatest interest to marketers.

Snapshot Countries by Region

1. United States	}	North America
2. France	⎫	
3. United Kingdom	⎪	
4. Spain	⎬	Western Europe
5. Germany	⎪	
6. Netherlands	⎭	
7. Turkey	⎫	
8. Russia	⎬	Eastern Europe
9. Ukraine	⎭	
10. Argentina	⎫	Latin America
11. Brazil	⎭	
12. India	}	India
13. China	}	China
14. Taiwan	⎫	
15. Hong Kong	⎪	
16. Japan	⎬	Asia Pacific
17. South Korea	⎪	
18. Australia	⎭	

Each section includes some relevant profile data, the percentage of teens in the six value segments, and some personal observations.

First, let's review the values segments again so you can make comparisons:

Segment	Percentage
Thrills and chills	18
Upholders	16
Quiet achievers	15
Resigned	14
Bootstrappers	14
World savers	12

Bear in mind that on a global basis the segments are roughly the same size. However, the skews by country are sometimes enormous.

And now let's zoom around the globe—something I am frequently doing in my quest to understand global youth culture.

Country 1: United States–Teen Mecca

Today's U.S. teen is racing toward the future and creating a different life from that of past generations. The key difference is that these teens are *doers*, action-oriented kids with a hands-on, can-do mentality. They are focused, ambitious, and self-confident, and the key underlining goal is to accomplish as much as possible.

U.S. kids would win a gold medal if being out at night were an Olympic event. The nation is comprised of social extroverts who

United States: Snapshot

19.6 million 15- to 19-year-olds
73 percent urban/suburban
96 percent middle class
100 percent teen literacy

United States: Segment Distribution	
SEGMENT	PERCENTAGE
Thrills and chills	28
Bootstrappers	26
Quiet achievers	10
Resigned	9
World savers	9
Upholders	7

like to spend time with friends at parties, the mall, school activities, or on dates. Other than working or playing on computers, U.S. teens rarely participate in solitary activities.

These outside social activities do take a toll, reducing the time U.S. teens spend reading, studying, or playing a musical instrument. The time given to play also contributes indirectly to the main worry, not getting good grades.

American teens are not as influenced by world cultures, which are often viewed as far away and exotic. These kids are insular, not seeing beyond the domestic borders of a nation that dominates a continent. The result is that without a marked world appreciation or world conscience, U.S. teens voice fewer concerns about global societal, environmental, and political problems.

Fast Facts about U.S. Teens

91 percent listen to music.
45 percent bowl, the highest-rated participatory sport.
41 percent say, "I am in love."
22 percent smoke.
12 percent study in their leisure time.

U.S. teens are the undisputed mediavores of the world. They plug in daily to a host of entertainment, news, and information choices. Radio and television dominate their media habits, but computers are fast becoming the new medium of choice.

It is important to note that the U.S. teen population will increase significantly over the next five years. Two media areas will be primarily influenced by the rise: the Internet, particularly music (and music is now the number-one reason why Americans go online), and movies. Regarding the latter medium, a larger universe of teen moviegoers will demand more teen-oriented films. These movies, in turn, will provide marketers piggyback or cross-promotional opportunities to climb on the summer movie bonanza bandwagon.

For U.S. teens, exposure to commercial messages begins at an early age, a benefit to marketers. American teenagers respond to promotions and advertising, especially on the local level.

In sum, U.S. teens are a highly content and optimistic group, despite whatever you might read in the newspaper about the troubled, alienated teens with guns. Those few individuals, like those who opened fire in Columbine High School, are seriously disturbed young adults. In no way do they reflect the true spirit of this optimistic new generation of Americans.

Country 2: France–Uncertainty and Skepticism

The great nation of France might be in difficulty in the future if its current alienated and cynical teenagers do not find a more pos-

---

France: Snapshot

4 million 15- to 19-year-olds
74 percent urban/suburban
55 percent middle class
99 percent teen literacy

France: Segment Distribution

SEGMENT	PERCENTAGE
Thrills and chills	24
Resigned	18
World savers	17
Quiet achievers	9
Upholders	7
Bootstrappers	4

itive worldview. When questioned about attitudes and values, French teens voice a pessimism about what the future holds in store. Only 27 percent agree with the statement, "I know that somehow or other I will have a good life," and a very low 16 percent agree that "The world will improve in my lifetime."

Judgmentally, the underlying reasons for these negative expressions stem from economic realities and from a national resistance to embrace new technology. Economically, high unemployment has driven many teenagers to other European countries to find work. On a recent trip to London, I discovered that a number of people behind the counter and waiting on tables were French youths. They had left France, which has a high unemployment rate.

Further, France is not as enthusiastic as other countries in embracing computers and the Internet, fearing that both are English-speaking, American-dominated entities. This commercial xenophobia inhibits French teenagers from joining in the teen technological revolution that is occurring globally.

This somewhat doom-and-gloom outlook reflects a disenchantment in which French teens rank wanting to fit into society low, at 25 percent, and only 14 percent rank upholding time-honored traditions, customs, and values as "very important."

Fast Facts about French Teens

82 percent like to spend time with friends.

71 percent own a good dress or suit (worldwide total is 62 percent).

64 percent prefer foreign movies.

60 percent drink bottled water, the highest total in the world.

53 percent smoke, 19 percent higher than the Western European average.

French teens, like teens worldwide, look to the United States for their fashion and culture, at 86 percent—interestingly, this splits as 90 percent for girls and 81 percent for boys. The United States is also the main destination target of French teens, at 37 percent, and 19 percent would like to reside in America.

French teens are less likely than teens worldwide to say they like to shop (47 versus 54 percent). Marketers take note: French teens are significantly less likely to admit to being influenced by advertising than the world average (11 versus 28 percent).

However, one way or another they find a way to acquire fashion. As consumers, French teens rank in the highest 10 percent worldwide at purchasing products. They buy jeans, athletic shoes, watches, and backpacks, all consumption at high Western European averages.

Since the future seems uncertain, French teens make the most of the here and now. They represent one of the highest percentages of thrills-and-chills teens in the world, at 34 percent. These kids are determined to have fun and enjoy themselves today. Friendships are important because pals are the conduit to having fun and going out.

The bottom line is that French teens feel powerless to effect change, and many have opted for an early acquaintance with hedonism. French teens live for today.

Country 3: United Kingdom—Friends and Family Ties Bind

British teens stand at the vanguard of a generational trend of self-reliance that also characterizes much of the teen world. 92 percent of all teens agree, "It's up to me to get what I want in life." This is a clear indication of the pragmatism that marks this can-do U.K. spirit.

The economic upheaval brought about by the Margaret Thatcher years is only a distant memory to these teens. They live in a nation currently enjoying widespread prosperity and one that offers a chance for a secure economic future.

The traditional benefits from the British welfare state coupled with a burgeoning economy have made the current teen genera-

United Kingdom: Snapshot

3.7 million 15- to 19-year-olds
92 percent suburban
96 percent middle class
99 percent teen literacy

United Kingdom: Segment Distribution

SEGMENT	PERCENTAGE
Thrills and chills	34
Resigned	21
World savers	14
Bootstrappers	9
Quiet achievers	8
Upholders	7

tion a carefree, devil-may-care one. More than 90 percent of these kids enjoy socializing with friends, whether it's watching television, having a pint at the pub, or going to a rock concert. British teens score near the high end of the scale in valuing "having as much fun as possible."

These teens are distinctly mediavores, scoring very high on watching television or reading newspapers. Marketers should take note: Newspapers are a highly viable way to advertise to British teens, as well as magazines. Some 57 percent of British teens read at least one magazine weekly, one of the highest totals in the world.

I was surprised at the very high level of importance placed on the family in the United Kingdom—60 percent considered this relationship paramount. These levels do not approximate the Asian totals, where family and work are paramount. Yet, more than 78 percent say they trust their parents in most cases, a marked increase over American teens, who do not rate parental trust as high.

Finally, British teens are megaconsumers, and most have money from work or family allowances to shop to the max. To witness this shopping frenzy, stand on Oxford Road in London on the May Bank Holiday weekend and watch as tens of thousands of British teens stream out of the department stores, their shopping bags filled with clothing, electronic equipment, and sports gear.

Fast Facts about British Teens

92 percent watch television daily.

82 percent read a daily or weekly newspaper, the highest total in the world.

61 percent of all males expect to live a better life than their parents.

57 percent drink beer or wine, versus 22 percent worldwide.

36 percent have cable television, 16 percent lower than the worldwide average.

The British teen balances goal attainment (i.e., a completed education and a good job) with family, friends, and fun. British teens are ready to move forward with confidence.

Country 4: Spain–Social Relationships

Spain is included in the Western European country snapshots to point out some small but significant differences among teens. At the outset, it should be stated that Spain has a 20 percent unemployment rate, which casts a cloud over its economic future. However, this Wave II study was conducted among middle-class teenagers who have higher prospects for the better jobs, and should therefore be the most optimistic.

Spain: Snapshot

2.7 million 15- to 19-year-olds
77 percent urban/suburban
91 percent middle class
99 percent teen literacy

Spain: Segment Distribution

SEGMENT	PERCENTAGE
World savers	24
Resigned	21
Thrills and chills	18
Upholders	12
Bootstrappers	9
Quiet achievers	7

Although their families are not as affluent as their French or British counterparts, Spanish teenagers enjoy a healthy measure of consumption. Compact disc players are found in 80 percent of homes, along with radios, at 99 percent.

Spanish teens are not avid technophiles—only 34 percent state that they have easy access to the new technology. In addition, only 25 percent have a computer with a modem at home. But again, these data come from middle-class students and do not reflect the national average.

The emergence of a new generation of women differentiates Spanish teens from those of other more-developed European countries. Females in Spain, finally, are starting to enjoy the same freedoms as males. In this regard, Spain seems more similar to emerging Asian and South American countries than to the rest of Western Europe.

Spanish female teens are on par with males in their desire to go to a university and get a good job. They also enjoy drinking wine and beer on equal levels (32 versus 33 percent), which contrasts with global drinking patterns that are highly skewed toward males.

The economic prospects for Spain are promising in light of the recent amalgamation of states into the European Union. Spain still has a lower labor rate than the northern countries, and forecasts are that industry will migrate south to take advantage of this

---

Fast Facts about Spanish Teens

93 percent enjoy spending times with friends, the highest total in the world.

80 percent are apprehensive about terrorism.

33 percent enjoy wine or beer.

18 percent expect to be famous.

6 percent anticipate they will work for the government.

cost differential. More employment will create new opportunities for the next generation of Spanish teens.

Teens in Spain are perhaps the most social in the world. They love to spend time with friends (93 percent versus 77 percent worldwide) and are keen party- and moviegoers.

For teen marketers, Spain will represent an increasingly more lucrative country during the next 10 years, with more product consumption. Teens in Spain enjoy strong governmental assistance, and the economic future seems bright.

Country 5: Germany–In Transition

When the Berlin Wall came down in 1989 two vastly different cultures merged, creating social uncertainty and lingering discontinuity. On one side there was the Western German culture, where teens are accustomed to one of the world's highest standards of living, and on the Eastern side teens accustomed to doing without from childhood. As a result there is a sharp distinction between the Western "haves" and the Eastern "have-nots."

The East falls short on basic telephone availability, computer access, and so on. Moreover, Easterners have yet to adjust their levels of optimism to reflect newly available possibilities. East German teens tend to worry more about nearly everything in their lives, from getting a good job, to AIDS and war, to finances and

Germany: Snapshot

4.5 million 15- to 19-year-olds
86 percent urban/suburban
95 percent middle class
99 percent population literacy

Germany: Segment Distribution

SEGMENT	PERCENTAGE
Thrills and chills	37
Resigned	27
World savers	11
Bootstrappers	9
Upholders	5
Quiet achievers	4

death. It will take time for the realization of new opportunities to take hold of this cohort's psyche.

In reaction to uncertainty, teens in Germany depend on relationships to forge their identities and create their own secure, happy environments. There is skepticism over the correlation between achievement and reward, despite a sense of responsibility for getting what they want in life.

In the short term, German teens are driven by fun and pleasure. This comes primarily from music and media entertainment of all sorts. When German teens go out, they are most likely to see a movie (60 percent), eat in a restaurant (30 percent), play pool (35

Fast Facts about German Teens

99 percent own a pair of blue jeans.

82 percent expect to be happy adults.

77 percent read magazines at least monthly.

14 percent expect to be respected in their communities, versus 54 percent worldwide.

13 percent are in love, versus 35 percent worldwide.

percent), or go to a concert (24 percent). At home, MTV music videos usually are a popular choice.

Overall, German teens are far less likely to attend university (29 percent, versus 72 percent worldwide), due to the highly competitive nature of the education system and the availability of alternative career options such as apprenticeships. The majority, however, expect to have a job they like (84 percent), find someone to love (82 percent), have a nice house or apartment (80 percent), and be happy as an adult (82 percent). Hence, the uncertainty on cultural, social, and political change has not eroded this nation's spirit of personal optimism for the long term, at least in what this generation believes matters. German teens do not expect to be rich (21 percent), be leaders in their communities (14 percent), or be better off than their parents (36 percent). What they do expect to attain will be enough to satisfy.

The availability of state-of-the-art technology to German teens at home gives them the highest levels of teen access to equipment worldwide in many categories, with the exception of online services. However, there remains a technological divide between East and West. Cable television access is 86 percent, versus 52 percent worldwide. Moreover, CD penetration is 91 percent, versus 62 percent globally. Computer access is in the average range (26 percent). However, use of computers presents a somewhat unique profile.

Despite heavy interest in computer games, German teens are far more likely than their counterparts in other countries to do adult-style work with databases and spreadsheets.

Finally, it should be noted that German teens are fascinated by the United States. Four out of every five German teens consider the United States to be the leader in fashion and teen lifestyles. German teens also like to travel, and the United States is their first choice of destination (40 percent), followed by Australia (11 percent) and Italy (9 percent).

German Teen Computer Usage

COMPUTER USES	GERMANY	GLOBAL AVERAGE
Basic access	26%	23%
Computer games	73	71
Word processing	58	46
Database utilization	44	20
Spreadsheet functions	27	15

Especially warm and sociable, German teens are for the most part coping well with change, managing their own expectations for the future, and successfully finding joy in each day.

Country 6: The Netherlands–Worldly and Wired

The Netherlands is the most densely populated country in Western Europe, with a booming economy. In fact, it has the world's ninth-largest gross domestic product. Culture in this country can be characterized by a cosmopolitan atmosphere, a liberal culture (known for tolerance regarding drugs and sex), and brisk international trade.

Netherlands: Snapshot

900,000 15- to 19-year-olds
89 percent urban/suburban
97 percent middle class
99 percent population literacy

Netherlands: Segment Distribution

SEGMENT	PERCENTAGE
Thrills and chills	32
Resigned	26
World Savers	10
Bootstrappers	10
Quiet achievers	7
Upholders	6

Dutch teens grow up fast, but not fast enough for their own lik-
ing. They possess a strong will to take on the responsibilities of
adulthood. They are self-directed workers who carefully plan for
the future. But at the same time, they balance their hard work with
fun and sociability. Individualism, outspokenness, and fairness are
strong values within their culture. As a result, Dutch teens are
unusually confident in their ability to create happy lives for themselves now and in years to come.

Happiness *now* comes from keeping active. Teens living in the
Netherlands are constantly in motion—playing sports, riding

Fast Facts about Netherlands Teens

93 percent watch television daily.

61 percent are saving money for the future, versus 37 percent
worldwide.

52 percent say they are in love.

34 percent plan to attend university, versus 72 percent worldwide.

14 percent worry about not living up to others' expectations, versus 27 percent worldwide.

bikes, shopping, dancing, and generally socializing. When they do stop to catch their breath, Dutch teens stay plugged into the world at large via television and computers (71 percent). Access to the Internet is relatively high, at 18 percent.

As consumers, Dutch teens are price conscious. Only 23 percent agree with the statement, "When I really want a brand, price doesn't matter." This does not stop them, however, from acquiring a full array of consumer goods, including ubiquitous ownership of jeans (93 percent) and athletic shoes (94 percent).

Travel is a top priority for the Dutch. More than a third of Dutch teens definitely plan to travel after graduating from high school, with the United States and Australia set as distant targets. 90 percent of Dutch teens consider the United States to be the leader in global teen fashion and culture.

Pessimistic about the world at large (only 11 percent believe the world will improve in their lifetime), Dutch teens believe it is up to them to get what they want in life. This is perhaps why they save money at much higher levels than average (61 percent, versus 37 percent worldwide), and over half have paying jobs (54 percent, versus 29 percent average for Western Europe).

Dutch teens represent a rare combination of maturity and joie de vivre. They can work hard, play hard, make money, save money, master technology, and be in love, all at the same time.

Country 7: Turkey–Gender Determination

Turkey is a fascinating country and one that holds many surprises for marketers. Traditionally, it is where East met West, and this continues to the present day. I wanted to include one predominantly Muslim country in this chapter, and Turkey qualifies on this account even though it is highly secular.

Another reason to cite Turkey is the wide disparity between genders. 74 percent of males are enrolled in secondary schools,

```
┌─────────────────────────────────────────┐
│          Turkey: Snapshot                │
│  ───────────────────────────────────     │
│  6.7 million 15- to 19-year-olds         │
│  67 percent urban/suburban               │
│  56 percent middle class                 │
│  60 percent inflation                    │
└─────────────────────────────────────────┘
```

compared to only 48 percent of females. This bias actively limits career opportunities for females, especially among the lower socio-economic classes.

The gender gap extends beyond attending school and leisure activities. Turkish female teens enjoy spending time with friends more than males do (88 versus 70 percent). In addition, these females enjoy talking on the telephone more than males (77 versus 34 percent). Finally, females enjoy going to parties more than males (41 versus 32 percent).

In fact, the cultural or religious line that separates the genders can also be expressed by the contrast in recreational interests: Turkish boys' participate in sports, versus Turkish girls' interest in the arts. In no other country in the Wave II study was this demarcation so evident.

Turkey: Segment Distribution

SEGMENT	PERCENTAGE
Thrills and chills	27
Resigned	21
World savers	12
Bootstrappers	10
Upholders	8
Quiet achievers	5

Fast Facts about Turkish Teens

64 percent go on dates, versus 34 percent globally.

65 percent attend a weekly religious service.

31 percent of males expect to join the military after high school.

44 percent strive to be accepted as an individual, versus 28 percent worldwide.

Specifically, these are the cultural and artistic differences that skew to females:

Listening to the radio: 75 percent for females versus 44 percent for males

Reading books: 73 percent for females versus 34 percent for males

Writing poetry, fiction, or in a journal: 48 percent for females versus 13 percent for males

But athletic pursuits are predominantly a male activity, as follows:

Watching sports: 62 percent for males versus 32 percent for females

Playing pool: 45 percent for males versus 21 percent for females

Playing sports: 68 percent for males versus 45 percent for females

One notable statistic is the enormous gap in computer usage: The total for working or playing with computers is 56 percent for males, compared with only 22 percent for females.

Nevertheless, Turkish females have bright expectations for their futures. Consider these two findings: 84 percent of Turkish female teens expect to be happy as adults, versus 65 percent of males, and 88 percent anticipate they will succeed in their careers, as opposed to the more doubtful males, at 77 percent.

Country 8: Russia—Change and Disillusionment

The disintegration of the former Soviet Union opened up economic opportunities in Russia, which then collapsed. The future is uncertain, and many U.S. entrepreneurs who went mining for gold have retrenched or are playing the waiting game. Ironically, one of the only businesses that has flourished has been matchmaking services for American men to meet Russian women.

Teens in Russia are naturally pessimistic about the future, especially in the wake of rampant crime, chronic unemployment, and economic uncertainty. Further, internecine miniwars between Russia and ethnic separatists in Chechnya and other regions paint a bleak picture.

Russian teens, living amid pollution, malnutrition, and alcoholism have put on a brave face, but, realistically, they are guarded and cautious about their prospects. While they are less likely than global teens to look forward to health and happiness, they do evince optimism about what they can control: social relationships.

The adage "safety in numbers" can describe how much Russian teens like to get together with friends (73 percent). Perhaps these teen years—still a long time away from adulthood and responsibilities—have fashioned a group-oriented "Let's party" mentality. These teens spend as much time out of the house as possible, playing pool (50 percent) or even strolling around town (32 percent).

Russia: Snapshot

11.9 million 15- to 19-year-olds
76 percent urban/suburban
88 percent middle class
99 percent teen literacy

Russia: Segment Distribution

SEGMENT	PERCENTAGE
World savers	20
Quiet achievers	18
Thrills and chills	16
Upholders	14
Resigned	12
Bootstrappers	10

Make no mistake, Russian teens like to shop, and most have some allowance money for small-ticket purchases. 72 percent state that they enjoy listening to CDs, tapes, or records, although CD ownership, at 22 percent, is substantially lower than the 62 percent total globally. 81 percent of females wash daily with soap or a facial cleanser.

But more than their world counterparts, Russian teens are openly disillusioned with traditional institutions. This understandable pessimism is reflected in the fact that they do not fore-

Fast Facts about Russian Teens

94 percent have an allowance, one of the highest totals in the world.

70 percent have a VCR.

48 percent do grocery shopping.

23 percent state that the world will improve in their lifetime.

14 percent are saving money for the future, versus 37 percent worldwide.

see living in a healthy environment and have only moderate expectations of living in a peaceful world.

Russia is another teen country that believes in living for today. And you can hardly blame these teens for that pleasure-seeking attitude. But these kids are resilient, and if there is an economic upturn in the country, Russian teens will find new ways to grab the gold ring.

Country 9: Ukraine–Optimism and Consumption

Ukraine is an example of an Eastern European country in the throes of an economic and political upheaval that, in contrast to Russia, is actually optimistic. But what makes this country so interesting are the high numbers for the purchase of typical teen cosmetic and body care products. In fact, these totals parallel America's.

The country has been independent from the Soviet Union since 1991. In these nine years of economic freedom, Ukraine has prospered commercially because of its historic production of grain and other crops. Agriculture hires 50 percent of the total workforce. There is a thriving industrial segment in the eastern part of the country.

The result today is that unemployment is less than 1 percent (one of the lowest totals in the world) but inflation is at 14 percent. When unemployment is so low, opportunities seem boundless, and this

---

Ukraine: Snapshot

3.7 million 15- to 19-year-olds
67 percent urban/suburban
80 percent middle class
97 percent teen literacy

Ukraine: Segment Distribution

Segment	Percentage
Quiet achievers	20
Thrills and chills	18
World savers	15
Bootstrappers	13
Upholders	12
Resigned	12

reflects why Ukrainian teens are so optimistic. In fact, Ukrainian teens believe they can have it all—complete their education, marry, and, for many, enjoy wealth—a statement not heard in Russia.

The rosy optimism stemming from a prosperous economy has produced other positive statements about the future. 87 percent state that they will find a job that they like, compared to 76 percent in Eastern Europe. And 78 percent think they will have career success, which is also higher than their neighbors' 67 percent.

Further, with the outlook bright in a job or career, materialistic optimism also prevails—88 percent of Ukrainian teens anticipate that they will live in a nice house or apartment, versus 73 percent globally.

Fast Facts about Ukrainian Teens

46 percent go to bars, versus 30 percent in Eastern Europe.
50 percent play cards, versus 36 percent worldwide.
77 percent of females date.
17 percent read newspapers.
61 percent have a college sweatshirt or T-shirt.

For me, the most important finding about Ukrainian teens is that 75 percent perceive that they will have a better life than their parents. This is 30 percentage points higher than the world average, and 21 points higher than Eastern Europe. As indicated earlier, Ukrainian teens also stand at the top of the world's teen dating order. Clearly, optimism and lack of economic fears contribute to this healthy dating environment.

Marketers not selling in Ukraine should reexamine their priorities. A heavy dating population of teens needs cosmetics, shampoos, clothing, and the accoutrements of entertainment.

Ukrainians are also in the position to serve as opinion leaders, as they are envied by other Eastern European teens.

Country 10: Argentina–The Worried Generation

Argentina represents a highly developed country whose teens reveal worries about almost everything. The question for marketers is why Argentinean teens exhibit such trepidation about the future. The answers are both economic and political. In Argentina, unemployment had been a comfortable 6.5 percent in 1991, and had almost doubled to 12 percent by the time of this study. Historically, a volatile economy sends teens' hopes up and down like a roller-coaster ride.

Politically, the South American continent has been moderately peaceful during the past decade, with the exception of the guer-

---

Argentina: Snapshot

3.3 million 15- to 19-year-olds
87 percent urban/suburban
84 percent middle class
97 percent literacy

Argentina: Segment Distribution

SEGMENT	PERCENTAGE
World savers	22
Resigned	21
Thrills and chills	17
Upholders	13
Bootstrappers	10
Quiet achievers	8

rilla movement roiling Colombia. But many of the other democra-cies rest on fragile ground, and left- or right-wing insurgencies could alter the calm landscape.

Argentine teen worries span education, career, family, personal, health, and even the environment. These worries are not just higher than worldwide totals, but also are marginally higher than those for other South American countries.

Teens in Argentina are significantly more likely to worry about finishing their education than are teens globally (72 versus 54 per-cent). In addition, they are more likely to worry about getting a good job (82 versus 70 percent).

Fast Facts about Argentine Teens

89 percent watch television daily.

69 percent worry that they will not find someone to love.

54 percent expect that they will live in Argentina as adults.

43 percent watch MTV and music videos, the highest total in South America.

35 percent believe they will be better off than their parents, versus 48 percent for Latin America as a whole.

But it is in the personal area that the greatest fears about self and relationships surface. My heart goes out to these teens who fear losing someone they love (79 percent, versus 57 percent globally), finding a place to live (61 percent, vs. 39 percent globally, versus 51 percent for Latin America), and not having friends (59 percent, versus 35 percent globally).

Even in the area of health, Argentine teens voice great concerns about the future. They worry about AIDS (79 percent, versus 43 percent globally), unplanned pregnancy (32 percent, versus 20 percent globally), and taking drugs (26 percent, versus 12 percent globally).

Historically, the years of civil war have engendered fears that such a bloody and divisive situation could return. Teens worry about becoming a victim of terrorism (51 percent, versus 24 percent globally, and 40 percent for Latin America) and being at war (60 percent, versus 33 percent globally), and the Falklands conflict continues to haunt the younger generation. Despite a high standard of living and a rich culture, for Argentinean teens, tomorrow is fraught with worries.

Country 11: Brazil–Party Time

It's party time for Brazil's 16 million teenagers. These are kids who really enjoy being young. In this highly urbanized country (77

Brazil: Snapshot

17.8 million 15- to 19-year-olds
77 percent urban/suburban
50 percent middle class
30 percent of population is ages 10 to 24

Brazil: Segment Distribution

SEGMENT	PERCENTAGE
World savers	24
Thrills and chills	17
Bootstrappers	15
Quiet achievers	12
Upholders	10
Resigned	8

percent urban or suburban), there are plenty of opportunities for being out of the house—and *out* is the place to be for teens who want to have a good time.

Judgmentally, the country's multiracial culture contributes to the sybaritic lifestyle. Everyone seems to get along, and there is no segregation of people by color. In my many trips to Brazil, I have been conscious of how unimportant race is to the people of this enormous country. This humanistic attitude flows down to the children and the teenagers.

Brazilian teens love music and going to clubs for dancing. They enjoy dancing, partying, and spending time with friends. They are

Fast Facts about Brazilian Teens

53 percent love to dance, versus 32 percent worldwide.
79 percent play soccer.
84 percent expect to attend university.
24 percent are saving money for the future.
95 percent own athletic shoes.

less likely than teens globally to spend time alone or doing solitary pursuits.

The favorite activity is listening to music: 81 percent say they like to listen to CDs, tapes, or records, and this is slightly above the worldwide average. But they enhance their music pleasure by listening to the radio at a rate higher than that of their global peers (76 versus 59 percent).

In their drinking habits, Brazilian teens are further advanced than other teens who live in more restricted societies: 43 percent of these teens go to bars, versus 19 percent globally. And their consumption of wine or beer is also significantly higher than the worldwide average (33 versus 22 percent).

Soccer is king in Brazil, with 79 percent teen participation (male and female), versus 67 percent worldwide. But other sports score much lower than global averages, including basketball, gymnastics, and tennis.

Without a lot of money to spend, Brazilian teens have opted to buy those things that go with partying outside the home, such as food and snacks, drinks, cigarettes, and concert tickets. These purchasing decisions have resulted in having less money to spend on personal care products. Females use significantly less mascara, eye liner and shadow, blush, or rouge than other teens—about 75 percent less. Males own fewer blazers, sweat shirts, or sports team jackets than their counterparts. But, then again, the climate is hot!

So, for Brazilian teens, life is a constant musical carnival.

Country 12: India–Cultural Mosaic

Indian society is so huge and complex that it is often difficult for marketers to envision succeeding there. This is why it is helpful to recognize that culturally, economically, and geographically, there are several Indias. The India that is most salient to marketers, especially foreign ones, is large, well-educated, and fairly well off.

India: Snapshot

101 million 15- to 19-year-olds
26 percent urban/suburban
58 percent below poverty line
52 percent adult literacy; rate growing among youth
$27.50 spending per week

If there are 101 million 15- to 19-year-olds, and only 25 percent of them are a reasonable economic target, then they still exceed the U.S. teen population in sheer target numbers. Looking at this smaller group of 25 million teens, we see a clear image of a well-educated, highly cultivated, deeply respectful, and thoughtful teen populace. Bootstrappers comprise the largest segment among Indian middle- to upper-class teens. This means they are serious about making a better life for themselves and are willing to work hard to get it.

While their Asian counterparts in Japan and Korea face overwhelming external pressure to excel at their school work, Indian

India: Segment Distribution

SEGMENT	PERCENTAGE
Bootstrappers	23
Upholders	19
Resigned	15
World savers	12
Quiet achievers	10
Thrills and chills	8

teens seem to genuinely enjoy learning new things, studying, and participating in a number of creative and artistic positions.

Perhaps some of India's strong religious beliefs defuse the potential tension between generations. Indian teens have a high regard for their parents and families. They are eager to please, and follow traditions without feeling they are sacrificing a satisfying life in the modern world.

As one teenaged Indian boy we interviewed in Bombay told us, "I love Indian values and traditions very much. I want to go to the top. I will have to fix an aim and work hard to achieve it. You must believe in yourself. Power and courage and confidence, if one has them, he can succeed." These words epitomize the values of the bootstrapper segment in India, where traditional family values are not in conflict with ambitions for the future.

What foreign marketers need to know about India is just how vibrant and modern Indian culture is for young people. Indian teens embrace culture of all kinds—reading, creative writing, movies, television, and music. In essence, the economically comfortable Indian teens are the epitome of balance in the way they approach the dual cultural passport. They are open to global culture but still retain a tremendous affection and sense of pride in their own local culture, both traditional and contemporary. Marketers who understand and respect these differences can offer products and services that will be integrated into the mix.

Fast Facts about Indian Teens

79 percent rely on parents' advice for products.

78 percent attend religious services.

20 percent have a CD player, versus 62 percent worldwide.

50 percent are concerned about poverty, versus 35 percent worldwide.

64 percent read a newspaper daily, versus 42 percent worldwide.

One final note about teen life in India: It is not a level playing field for boys and girls. Girls have far more responsibility for household chores and far less freedom over their own future than anyone else in the world. As one Indian girl told me, "Even if I study for ten years, I have to do the household work. My parents say you are a woman and you have to do all the work. I want to enjoy life, but I don't want to hurt my parents." This girl is a typical upholder, the second-largest segment in India.

Country 13: China–The New Frontier

Nothing fascinates me more than Chinese teens. This is because they are so much like Americans in their ambitions, and yet so unique in their new experience with capitalism. For Westerners it is difficult to picture a world where until recently everyone was in uniform, women wore no makeup, and the freedom to make personal choices, from choosing a career to having a child or traveling abroad, was controlled by the state.

Now that the electricity has been turned on, metaphorically, the Chinese teen is dazzled by the Technicolor possibilities. Modern Chinese culture is a fascinating paradox of traditional values and foreign influence. Bowling alleys, discos, and bumper cars are

---

China: Snapshot

98 million 15- to 19-year-olds, 5 times the number of teens in the
  United States
31 percent urban/suburban
48 percent middle class or above
95 percent teen literacy, primarily Mandarin

China: Segment Distribution	
SEGMENT	PERCENTAGE
Quiet achievers	44
Upholders	29
Bootstrappers	8
Thrills and chills	5
World savers	4
Resigned	3

all thriving among urban youth and young adults with money. Fashion is sophisticated; hopes and dreams stretch far.

What I love about Chinese teens the most is their positive attitude and optimism. They know that the world is changing rapidly before their eyes, more so than for the rest of us. And yet their values stay solidly centered around family respect, honor for self and others, and achievement. More than anywhere else in the world, teens in China believe that the world will improve in their lifetime, because the world has amazingly improved already. Chinese teens are also more likely than average to believe it is up to them to get what they want in life. No free rides from government. No fatalistic sense of predestination. Chinese teens are ready and willing to work hard, stay true to their values, and reach for the stars. This is why almost half of them (44 percent) are quiet achievers.

Advertising and marketing to Chinese teens is one of the utmost challenges. This is because there is so little understanding among Western marketers about Chinese culture on the whole, and specifically Chinese youth culture. Only 13 percent of Chinese teens date in the Western context. Virtually no one goes to bars or smokes cigarettes. Having a job is nearly nonexistent (5 percent), although almost everyone gets an allowance.

Fast Facts about Chinese Teens

90 percent enjoy watching television.

84 percent enjoy basketball.

77 percent say they try to get access to technology as soon as they can.

74 percent enjoy reading, versus 51 percent worldwide.

69 percent believe the world will improve in their lifetime, versus 30 percent worldwide.

So where is the fun? Partly, the answer lies in the ubiquity of television, VCRs, DVDs, and music. Perhaps the greatest hunger among Chinese youth is for knowledge and cultural experience above and beyond material things.

Brands are not yet so important or established. Essentially, there are two spheres of influence on brands and fashion: local Chinese culture, from Shanghai, Beijing, and Hong Kong, as well as external marketing influences, especially from the United States, as well as from France and Japan. This constitutes another example of the dual cultural passport, which is manifest in fashion, music, food, and movies. Favorite sports, as elsewhere, are led by basketball and soccer.

While Chinese teens may be relatively childlike compared to their Western counterparts with respect to sexual relations, financial independence, and so on, they manifest an admirable maturity in their wisdom about life. Most exercise regularly, use computers, read newspapers or watch the news, enjoy time with friends and family, and have high expectations for a happy adult life.

While the world of capitalism and global media may be new, marketers to teens should never underestimate the ability of Chinese teens to make informed, wise decisions about brands.

Because of youth's dominance in this country, almost any marketer who wants to succeed in China needs to understand Chinese teens.

Country 14: Taiwan—Modern Traditionalism

Taiwan, like Hong Kong, is an island populated by ethnic Chinese. Economically prosperous and well educated, the Taiwanese teen has perhaps the least traditional of Chinese cultures. The big difference with Taiwanese teens is that almost 1 out of 3 is a thrills-and-chills or resigned type of kid.

Although Taiwanese teens hold their families in high regard, they may not think their parents share their tastes when it comes to consumer goods. About half of Taiwanese teens say they like to shop, and almost half (46 percent) say they become more interested in brands if they have good advertising (versus only 28 percent globally). Far fewer Taiwanese teens rely on their parents' advice for products (40 percent, versus 57 percent globally).

With consumerism in their blood, almost all Taiwanese teens own the global teen uniform of blue jeans, T-shirt, a wristwatch, athletic shoes, and a backpack. They are also highly likely to have a blazer, a denim jacket, and a sports team jacket, far more so than the global average.

Taiwan: Snapshot

1.9 million 15- to 19-year-olds
78 percent urban/suburban
87.5 percent of urban/suburban population in middle class
94 percent of males and 98 percent of females enrolled in secondary school

Taiwan: Segment Distribution

SEGMENT	PERCENTAGE
Upholders	31
Resigned	17
Thrills and chills	13
Bootstrappers	10
Quiet achievers	6
World savers	3

Where the Taiwanese teen varies from the rest of the world is in lower usage of the female accoutrements, including dresses, earrings, perfume, and especially makeup. What an opportunity for Cover Girl, Revlon, Avon, and L'Oreal!

Given that Taiwanese teens watch television and read the newspaper daily, it is most likely only a matter of time until they develop an interest in Western feminine fashion. Taiwanese teens already consider the United States to be a major influence on local culture and fashion, followed by Japan.

For most other aspects of their lifestyle, Taiwanese teens are plugged into the global teen culture. They are optimistic, education-

Fast Facts about Taiwanese Teens

91 percent have a VCR.

75 percent own a sports team sweatshirt or T-shirt, versus 37 percent worldwide.

52 percent are saving for the future.

13 percent use antiperspirant or deodorant, versus 65 percent worldwide.

3 percent work to earn money

focused, tech-savvy media enthusiasts, like most kids their age. Interestingly, they have a higher regard for the quality of education they receive than do their Hong Kong and mainland Chinese counterparts. Moreover, they are more environmentally concerned than the average teen, with their attention focused on the destruction of rain forests and on the environment in general.

Country 15: Hong Kong—Worldly Consumerism

Hong Kong teens are like rich relations to mainland China. Ethnically Chinese with many cultural similarities, Hong Kong teens have grown up on a small island that represents a high standard of living and a shopper's paradise. Shopping centers are abundantly stocked with high-end, costly brands and shining chrome escalators. Every block appears to sell Japanese electronics, European leather, world-class jewels, and American fast food. Hong Kong teens have grown up in the midst of one huge, well-stocked, glittering shopping center.

The standard of living is high, with 90 percent of the population middle class or better. Highly Westernized, having grown up in a long-established international financial center, many of Hong Kong's top students are setting their sights on business degrees and the golden ring.

Hong Kong: Snapshot

447,000 15- to 19-year-olds
95 percent urban/suburban
90 percent middle class or above
Nearly 100 percent teen literacy, with compulsory education to
   age 15

Hong Kong: Segment Distribution

SEGMENT	PERCENTAGE
Upholders	31
Resigned	17
Thrills and chills	13
Bootstrappers	10
Quiet achievers	6
World savers	3

Hong Kong teens vary from their mainland counterparts in a few other important ways. First, they are more comfortable with their Cantonese descent, even though about half speak Mandarin. Second, they are worried about the impact of Chinese government control. Hence, personal freedom is an important theme.

Moreover, because the standard of living is so high, Hong Kong teens have an abundance of technology at their fingertips. Most have a television, telephone, radio, audiocassette or CD player, and VCR. More than half use a computer weekly (57 percent), and the majority of computer users have them at home (81 percent).

Fast Facts about Hong Kong Teens

90 percent expect to attend university.
61 percent like to go shopping.
59 percent read comic books.
57 percent of females worry about being too fat.
51 percent fear loss of personal freedom.
Only 7 percent enjoy dancing.

With so much cultural sophistication and access to the world's marketplace, Hong Kong teens remain true to family values. Education is a top priority, and Hong Kong teens are serious minded about getting ahead. Like many Asian teens today, they are prepared to delay gratification for a rosy future and are not inclined to be seduced by risky pleasures of the moment.

With so much abundance and a good education, Hong Kong teens are far more optimistic than the worldwide average. The vast majority of them expect to be happy, healthy, prosperous adults with high-end lifestyles of their own making.

This is so important for marketers to understand. Like their counterparts in many regions of the world, Hong Kong teens are far from rebellion or cynicism. While they may be more open to expressing their individuality in fashion, the underlying value structure centers on respect for family and the drive to achieve.

Country 16: Japan—The Big Squeeze

Japanese teens live a squeezed life. Japan is approximately the size of California, with a population that is about half that of the entire United States. The majority (77 percent) live in urban areas where population density is extremely high and living accommodations are small.

Beyond the physical squeeze, Japanese youth feels pressure from enduring one of the most grueling educational systems in the

---

Japan: Snapshot

7.7 million 15- to 19-year-olds
77 percent urban/suburban
94 percent middle class
99 percent population literacy

Japan: Segment Distribution

SEGMENT	PERCENTAGE
Resigned	38
Thrills and chills	24
Quiet achievers	9
World savers	4
Bootstrappers	4
Upholders	7

world. From an early age, many students prepare for university entrance exams that will largely determine their futures. Approximately 60 percent of the members of each graduating class are admitted to college on the first try. Another 15 percent keep trying.

The squeeze further extends to rigid gender roles and uncertain futures. Most young women give up their jobs upon marrying. Young men face enormous pressure to fulfill their parents' dreams and expectations. Expectations among teens themselves are relatively bleak. There is a sense that the economy is troubled and job prospects are uncertain, and there is a fear of ultimately downgraded lifestyles. Very few Japanese teens expect to be better off than their parents (17 percent, versus 46 percent worldwide).

Fast Facts about Japanese Teens

67 percent read newspapers daily, versus 42 percent worldwide.
60 percent enjoy shopping, versus 44 percent worldwide.
57 percent never use a computer, versus 13 percent worldwide.
8 percent worry about poverty for others, versus 35 percent worldwide.
6 percent go to parties, versus 41 percent worldwide.

Moreover, only 10 percent agree that the world will improve in their lifetime.

This type of pressure-cooker situation gives rise to needs for release. Prominent values segments of the resigned (38 percent) and thrills-and-chills teens (24 percent) make youth culture in Japan far more like that of the Western European teens than that of the rest of Asia. Japanese youth, more so than most of their global cohorts, seek outlets for enjoyment and lean toward rebellion.

On a brighter front, Japanese teens enjoy living in the second-largest economy in the world. Despite recent downturns, Japanese teens continue to enjoy a high standard of living with an abundance of entertainment electronics at home.

The startling news is that computer access is very low in Japan compared to the global teen average. I am told that there are many reasons for this. First, Japanese education favors traditional methods, and therefore computers are not yet standard school equipment. Second, Japanese-language word processing is difficult, and software is relatively limited and expensive. Household penetration of computers is relatively low.

Japanese Teen Electronics Ownership

EQUIPMENT	PERCENTAGE
Television	100
Telephone	98
CD player	97
VCR	96
Radio	95
Audiocassette player	93
Video games	43
Computer	28

As consumers, the Japanese teens are serious shoppers. They are more brand-conscious than price-conscious, participating in a multitude of product categories. Worth noting is their high involvement with hair care products, health and beauty products, cosmetics, snacks, and video games.

Perhaps the most important source of pleasure (and solace) for Japanese teens is their relationships with friends. Like teens everywhere, the Japanese enjoy television daily. Unlike many other teens, they are avid readers of newspapers and magazines.

All told, Japanese teens have the benefit of a great standard of living. What they seek is a release from pressure and broader options for adult success.

Country 17: South Korea–Big "Little Tiger"

South Korean kids live amid strong economic growth, a high level of industrialization, and a rising standard of living. As in Japan, there is fierce competition for university spots, and intensive studying begins early. This is probably why such a large proportion of the population belongs to the resigned segment. These are the kids who largely do not expect to get into university and feel socially and economically stuck at a very young stage in life.

South Korea: Snapshot

3.8 million 15- to 19-year-olds.
80 percent urban/suburban
86 percent middle class
96 percent teen literacy
Average weekly spending $20
Annual teen spending $3.4 billion

South Korea: Segment Distribution

SEGMENT	PERCENTAGE
Resigned	40
Thrills and chills	19
Quiet achievers	19
Upholders	6
Bootstrappers	6
World savers	2

Clearly, the greatest emphasis among South Korean teens is on educational achievement. This is the main responsibility and focus of those teens who have not given up. Their parents support their efforts, providing them with computer equipment at home and relieving them of other responsibilities, such as household chores and earning money. South Korean teens—both males and females—are optimistic about their opportunities and the future. While they like to have fun, fewer say they engage in many of the social activities that take up the time of many teens worldwide. School is job one.

South Korean teens are success oriented and expect to rely on themselves to get what they want. Many are self-navigators with a true entrepreneurial drive. However, connections with others—friends, family, and society—remain very important. It may be that in the South Korea of today—a society that is undergoing rapid economic growth—it is necessary to achieve to truly fit in. Hence, South Korean teens struggle with the paradox of needing to excel as an individual in order to conform. This, in turn, creates tension and potential alienation among the teens who fear they can never measure up to their parents' dreams and expectations.

Keeping on the fast track in a fast-moving and changing society requires knowing what's happening. More than most teens world-

---

Fast Facts about South Korean Teens

98 percent are expected to get good grades.
98 percent wear jeans.
95 percent have a VCR.
82 percent have a CD player.
28 percent say they are happy most of the time.
1 percent worry about unplanned pregnancy.

---

wide, South Korean teens watch the news on television and read newspapers. They are looking for a competitive edge.

On the other hand, life is not economically hard for most South Korean teens. South Korean teens appear to be materially privileged, and they own a vast array of communications equipment. Many have a computer at home, even though they tend to have computers at school. More South Korean teens than the worldwide average own CD players and computers with modems and have access to online services. In addition, many own a good deal of casual sports clothing and are influenced by fashions from both the United States and Japan. It is likely that advertising and marketing programs developed in either Japan or the United States would translate well to South Korean youth culture.

Country 18: Australia—The Good Life

What is so refreshing about Australian teens is their positive outlook on the enjoyment of life. Australian teens are active, plugged into entertainment, and ready to laugh at the absurdities and amusements provided by their upbeat world.

Perhaps being cut off from the rest of the continent has made Australian teens determined not to lose touch. This is partly why

Australia: Snapshot

1.3 million 15- to 19-year-olds
85 percent urban
95 percent middle class or above

they embrace the Internet, go to the movies avidly, watch television, travel, and experience the world as fully as time and money permit.

Australian youths are sports and exercise fanatics. Never far from sunlight, the outdoors, and beaches, Australian teens of both genders are involved in sports and a have a broad, active lifestyle.

This is not to say, however, that Australian teens are not self-reliant, responsible or hard working. On the contrary, they plan for the future, desire to be respected for their individuality, and expect to make their own road in life. Top worries hinge on getting a good job (79 percent), having enough money (69 percent), and finishing their education (64 percent).

The optimistic worldview of Australian teens is no doubt fueled by a healthy economy, a high standard of living, and a sense of

Australia: Segment Distribution

SEGMENT	PERCENTAGE
Thrills and chills	22
Bootstrappers	17
World savers	16
Resigned	14
Upholders	8
Quiet achievers	5

Fast Facts about Australian Teens

93 percent enjoy comedy.
90 percent consider the United States to be the leader in fashion.
55 percent have a paying job.
35 percent had a chocolate bar today.
34 percent have access to a credit card.

being protected from some of the mainstream worries of more populated continents,—war, pollution, and AIDS. In other words, Australia appears to enjoy many of the benefits of modern society with fewer of its ills.

Australian teens want to have as much fun as they can. They fuel this fun and their aversion to boredom by being active in a full array of leisure activities, from parties (74 percent), to watching movies at home (71 percent), playing sports (65 percent), and eating out (52 percent).

Because Australian teens are so plugged into the world at large, they can be reached with mainstream U.S. and European marketing appeals. However, trend watchers should keep an eye on Australian teens, since their spirited individualism is apt to be a source of creativity and influence felt worldwide. Stated another way, Australian teens actively utilize both sides of their dual cultural passport.

8

How Marketers Can Tap into the $100 Billion Allowance

With insight into this new global generation, marketers can expand their brands into opportunity markets such as China, India, and Indonesia, as well as grow brand share and loyalty throughout the rest of the world. What is required is an in-depth assessment to identify the common leverage points between brand values and target values. Applying the analytic discipline that follows, marketers can assess how the unifiers of the generation can be leveraged to communicate brand appeal, where the differentiators need to be addressed for adjustment to marketing communications, and what the geographic cultural terrain is like to navigate. From this assessment springs understanding and creativity that works. But before I take you through the recommended approach, let's examine how some of the master marketers I have had the good fortune to work with firsthand make success happen within the teen target group.

Coca-Cola®, the World's Premier Marketer

The Coca-Cola Company ranks as the number-one marketer in the world. If you can take just one or two lessons from The Coca-Cola Company's international teen playbook, you will have a leg up on your competitors.

One of the most brilliant marketers I have had the pleasure to see in action is Sergio Zyman, formerly chief marketing officer at Coca-Cola, and famous for making marketing history with the introduction of Diet Coke®, as well as infamous for the earlier introduction of "New Coke®." Sergio often states, as he does in his recent book *The End of Marketing as We Know It* (HarperCollins, 1999), that "Marketing is not magic," and that "There's nothing mysterious about it." The sustained global success of The Coca-Cola Company comes from a consistent commitment to understanding the consumer on a global and local level. Where the company is innovative is often in its approach to obtaining that information. The other thing that is so impressive to me about The Coca-Cola Company is its wisdom in questioning the relevance of just about anything that happens anywhere to opportunities for its brands.

Because the prevalent attitude at Coca-Cola is that minor or major global news stories will be either advantageous or disadvantageous to the company, Coca-Cola operates a trend department that deals exclusively with monitoring worldwide lifestyles and events. It's a little like a commodity operation that scrutinizes the weather globally, recognizing that changes will have an impact on crops and crop prices. The main difference is that the crops the Coca-Cola trend department measures are values, lifestyles, and public opinion.

In 1997, when Princess Diana died in a car crash in Paris, the company added this significant event into its trend analysis because Coca-Cola realized that the soft drink market could be affected by the tragedy. I can't tell you what strategies—if any—

came out of this analysis, but I do know that Coca-Cola was probably the only consumer marketer to even consider the ramifications of this event on its brands.

Coca-Cola is interested in possible changes in attitude because the bottom line is that it has a passion to know what its customers feel every day. Coca-Cola wants to be able to harness worldwide events to promote the brand, and it relies heavily on trend data to make these decisions.

The Icon Triumphs

Coca-Cola excels at reaching teens via the dual cultural passport route, more than any other marketer I've encountered. For instance, on the global level, Coca-Cola advertises and promotes the Olympics, pairing its distinctive logo with the familiar five Olympic rings. On the local level of the cultural passport route, it sponsors local athletic events down to the village and school level.

The brand also plays to its historic strength in regions around the world where it arrived on the scene years earlier than Pepsi®. It considers each new generation as important as the last and will compete valiantly with challengers.

On a trip to Caracas, Venezuela, for Coca-Cola, I talked to scores of teenagers about the meaning of baseball in their lives and to their country. Coca-Cola was determined to connect with youth on a local unifier that was truly meaningful to its target's lives.

Coca-Cola promotes local athletics worldwide, whether it's street basketball in the outskirts of Manila, Philippines, or a Saturday college football program in the United States. Coca-Cola is able to build a global brand by reaching out to consumers at the local level.

The Icon Falters

In the early 1990s, Coca-Cola's marketers were stunned to realize that many members of the worldwide teen generation had no cognizance of the rich history and values of the brand. This was not just true in lesser-developed countries where the soft drink had only recently been introduced—it was also true even in the most developed markets, such as the United States. Most baby boomers may remember the multinational crowd of kids singing "I'd like to buy the world a Coke" on the hilltop—and the global values it engendered. But this new generation of Coca-Cola drinkers was not born when so many of the rich, major brand equity icons were established.

The meaning was clear: Coca-Cola needed to reconnect to the next generation. But to teens, Coca-Cola wasn't symbolic of a magnificent heritage, it was just a leading soft drink, lined up on the store shelves with all the others.

This was an opportunity to be seized. The company decided to reconnect the new generation with authentic Coca-Cola values. The first step was to bring back the Coca-Cola Contour Bottle, the signature sign-off used in decades of four-color magazine print ads. It also advertised the "fountain freshness" of its taste to a generation of fast-food enthusiasts who had never ordered a Coca-Cola from an old-style luncheonette. All of the ads and the promotion trumpeted one message: Coke® is authentic. "Always Coca-Cola."

Here's the important lesson from this tale: A marketer cannot assume that teenagers have any reference to a product's image, values, or icons other than those communicated within their lifetime. For teenagers, this means within the last 10 years. For each new generation, the relationship must begin anew.

Over time, Coca-Cola has reconnected to its teen base country by country. Today, the brand is the number-one most recognized logo in the world. It is also the number-one soft drink among teens in Africa, the Asia Pacific region, Canada, Eastern Europe, India, Latin America, the Middle East, the United States, and Western Europe.

Points to remember: Connect locally and globally, and make no assumptions regarding knowledge about your brand among today's teens.

Calvin Klein: Being Real

Remember the scene in *Back to the Future* when the befuddled Marty McFly awakens to discover he's been transported back to his own mother's teenage bedroom? And she, having peeked at his underwear to discover the mysterious stranger's name, calls him Calvin Klein. Talk about instant name recognition on a global basis.

In the early 1990s, Calvin Klein succeeded in selling its ready-to-wear clothing to teenagers because of an in-your-face ad campaign that depicted real kids in real situations. The ads did not airbrush out reality.

Teenagers responded to the imagery of true-to-life nonmodels. The brand was able to leverage its honest, no-bull approach by depicting some aspects of youth that were sexy and edgy. Some of the kids had zits and looked as if they hadn't had enough sleep after a night of partying. And eroticism loomed large. But they looked true to the target thrills-and-chills and resigned teens— they may not have been ready for an afternoon of tennis at the country club like Ralph Lauren models, but they were beautiful all the same.

Many critics complained about the clothing's sexual overtones and hurled accusations of heroin chic at the graphic print ads. But from a marketer's perspective, the clothier's frankness in dealing with the target's true-to-life self-image marked an honesty that teens embraced. The brand was cool.

The message was that teens could look sexy in Calvin Klein clothing, and the message was no different from that of past jeans advertising. It was just more in your face.

I'm convinced that teens responded positively to the campaign in part because the advertiser treated them as adults. These were no "wink, wink, nod, nod" ads—no coy handholding of young lovers on a mossy riverbank.

Calvin Klein understands that today's youth is immersed in the harsh realities of everyday life. These teens are exposed to an avalanche of news, much of it bad. They are often confronted daily with moral and ethical decisions about drugs, sex, and violence on the school grounds. They are therefore sometimes intolerant of sugar-coated portrayals in advertising that don't ring true to reality.

So much of what is positive about this generation is its ability to cope with reality in a positive way. When marketers treat youth with respect, acknowledging what is real, they in turn earn its respect and trust. In no way is this to suggest that commercials have to be graphically sexy or bleak in outlook. But an honest message suggests that your product will be reliable as well.

Point to remember: Teenagers respond well to honesty and realism. If your target teens are in an adultlike segment, treat them as young adults.

The National Basketball Association (NBA): Urban Roots and Heroes

One of the big surprises to many of my clients is that the NBA enjoys such passionate teen fan support outside of North America. We are inwardly focused when it comes to our homegrown American sports of baseball, football, and basketball. But the world has become more cohesive athletically. This was demonstrated in 1999 when the U.S. women's soccer team won the International Federation of Football Associations (FIFA) Women's World Cup in the Rose Bowl. If you can overcome the surprise of seeing millions of Americans watching women's soccer in the United States, then the leap to the popularity of basketball worldwide is effortless.

The NBA should serve as a marketing model for all products or brands that want to appeal to teens worldwide. It doesn't hurt that their product is great entertainment—fast-paced, colorful, and filled with enough heroes for everyone's taste. Equally important, the league's executives are savvy marketers who understand the sport's universal appeal.

The NBA realized that it could reach fans internationally by promoting its logo. The familiar signage became a visible part of every article of clothing the NBA promoted around the globe. The logo is exhibited prominently during the broadcast of each NBA game. Over time, the game and the logo became one.

Among global teens, basketball ranks first as the sport with the greatest involvement, meaning playing, watching live, and watching on television. Why the great appeal of NBA basketball outside of the United States? One reason is that girls count. Remember: Girls love basketball. It's their number-one most favored sport worldwide.

Another reason is Michael Jordan. For many years, he *was* the NBA. He became the world's first electronic sports hero whose popular icon status surpassed all boundaries. Jordan became larger than life, and his NBA career history read like that of a hero in a fairy tale. The other message from Jordan to teens worldwide was that you, too, could be rich and famous, starting when you're young.

Teens' Favorite Sports Involvement

Region	Number 1	Number 2
Africa	Basketball	Tennis
Asia Pacific	Basketball	Soccer
Canada	Basketball	Hockey
China	Basketball / soccer*	Tennis
Eastern Europe	Basketball	Soccer/tennis*
India	Cricket	Tennis
Latin America	Soccer	Basketball
Middle East	Basketball	Soccer
United States	Basketball	Football
Western Europe	Soccer	Basketball / tennis*

*Tied.

How did millions of teens become enamored with Jordan and the NBA? CNN brought the NBA into millions of homes worldwide with cable. Teens could watch the night's highlights in English.

The NBA tends to its international franchise by conducting clinics throughout the world. The players are sent out as ambassadors of the sport, giving instruction to boys and girls. Many marketers have used these NBA international basketball clinic as vehicles on which to piggyback their promotions and product giveaways.

Finally, basketball meets teens' longing for instant success. It's quick and high scoring, and so there's always some kind of achievement on the court. The fast pace of basketball resembles the fast action of kids' video games. Thus the craving for speedy stimuli feeds into the experiential hunger of computer-game-playing teenagers.

Point to remember: Teenagers respond favorably to action stimuli, rally around unifiers, and need positive heroes.

MTV: The Three Rs—Rhythm, Research, and Repetition

MTV is visual radio for young people. It takes the auditory pleasure of music and doubles it with visual movement.

Also, think of MTV as a mammoth global railroad system with miles and miles of railroad track that enters into millions of teen households. Not only does it carry its own products on the track, it also transports the messages of global and local brands via ads and promotions.

Did I say one track into each household? I meant two, because of the dual cultural passport mechanisms. The fact is, MTV is one of the best leveragers of the dual cultural passport among youth marketers.

MTV realized that to be successful it had to deliver a balance of international music programming (the global, upper roadway, and faster route) and national stars (the local, lower roadway, and slower route). So it set up operations in every country to realize the global/local concept.

Research—and MTV excels at research—said kids want to connect to the international pop icons but also want to see local music talent. So it should be no surprise that there's an MTV Mandarin operation in China, an MTV Madras that broadcasts in India, or an MTV Brazil that is customized to the Latin sound. MTV understands how to connect on a global and local basis.

In every hour of programming, kids in each country see a mix of U.S. or British videos and local videos. The percentage is adjusted by the demands of the marketplace. In China, MTV was initially licensed to broadcast only one hour a day.

Now for the most important fact about MTV, which may scare many baby-boomer marketers in the United States: MTV hires young executives (under 40) and gives them wide-ranging decision-making responsibilities.

This makes sense! One of the most glaring oversights among global marketers is not hiring young people to research and sell and market to other young people. Older experts can also be effective, but it helps to have some younger professionals to bridge the gap.

If you want to capture the youth market, you have to think young. Moreover, you have to *know* young. If you're age 40, 45, or older, you don't instinctively know what it's like to be a teenager or young adult in the world today. But someone age 20 or 25 is closer to the core.

MTV is also smart in hiring popular young *local* VJs to introduce the tunes. It always makes sure it includes VJs from the local region. It researches the right mix of international and local videos. It follows up in the field, doing research to gauge viewer reaction. And it repeats today's hits often so kids can enjoy the tops of the pops.

Points to remember: Hire young people who know their peers, do lots of research, and aim for a mix of local and global relevance.

Philips: Reaching Out to a New Generation

The challenge to Philips Electronics was threefold. The first issue was how to approach young people in the United States, where virtually no teenager had ever heard of Philips before. The second issue was a problem that many marketers may face in due course: how to change a somewhat stodgy image in the rest of the world, where the brand is a well-known household name. And the third issue was how to connect with a new generation of youth while staying poignant to older generations.

Such an ambitious undertaking required a strong commitment to consumer understanding. Philips embarked on a global study of consumers and their relationships with electronics and technology. We visited 14,000 homes in 17 countries, interviewing consumers as young as 15 and as old as 75. What we needed to understand most were the following points:

- What drives people in their quest for new technology products? (That is, what are the unifiers?)
- What key segments exist that may need to be addressed separately or with special lines or products? (That is, what are the key differentiators?)
- What does the Philips brand mean to people across segments and cultures? (That is, what are the brand values that need to be communicated through products and advertising?)

At the end of this ambitious international research undertaking, Philips had the strategic ammunition to develop a successful global advertising campaign that addressed all three challenges. Here's some of what we discovered, particularly as it relates to youth marketing:

- Throughout much of the world, young people are ambassadors of technology and change to older generations. Young people serve as aspirational role models in reverse. They easily grasp new technological concepts and hold the promise to living more enabled lives. They are eager to be the early adopters of new electronics products, and they do their homework to find the best brands. These young, savvy consumers epitomize the enlightened electronics consumer.

- The already established positioning for Philips's "Let's Make Things Better" campaign strikes a deep emotional chord across generations. The purpose of technology is to improve life in the areas we all care about: entertainment, time saving, communication, productivity, and self-enhancement. For Philips to stake this claim and live up to it means that the brand is addressing a relevant unifier that cuts across generations and regions.

- Successful advertising needs to teach by example. You cannot just *say* you are cool, you have to *be* cool. Moreover, you cannot just say you are state of the art in technology or making life better, you have to show it. In the packaged goods marketing world of Procter & Gamble, this means using a product demo to illustrate how Pampers helps babies stay drier or how Crest fights cavities. With electronics, it means that Philips has to demonstrate its star products, such as flat-screen television or CD recorders, and show how people's lives are enhanced by using them.

With these and other insights, Philips developed a global campaign through Messner Vetere Berger McNamee Schmetterer/Euro RSCG showcasing its star products, casting Philips tribe members, and presenting usage scenarios that are aspirational and involving. To underscore the unifying brand positioning of the "Let's Make Things Better" campaign, Philips utilized the Beatles song "Getting Better" to create an anthem of hope and possibilities the world over.

After one year, the results have been magnificent. The campaign put Philips on the map in the United States, where awareness grew from 55 to 80 percent among consumers under 25. Young adults now know from the start that the brand is cool. Worldwide, the brand has enjoyed increased sales as well as significant strides in brand consideration and imagery.

What was the secret of this success? There is no secret, as Sergio Zyman says. Philips did its homework, fully assessed its brand values, and linked them with the wants and needs of the global consumer. Stated more simply, Philips played the unifiers that in this case not only unified the youth generation but connected the brand to adults, as well. These unifiers were:

- Real-looking casting
- Cool star-product technology
- Humor and fun
- Hopeful, optimistic worldview

Moreover, Philips customized the campaign with regional executions and casting where appropriate in Asia and Europe. This means it took into consideration key differentiators to maximize communication success.

Point to remember: Research your consumer, and then apply the relevant target unifiers and differentiators.

So there you have it—five examples of global leaders I worked with personally who leveraged a deep understanding of New World Youth to their successful advantage.

Now let's examine step by step how you can do it, too.

How to Begin to Approach Global Youth: 12 Steps to Success

The information provided in this book will help you avoid reinventing the wheel. You are already equipped with a broad understanding of the global youth target. Now you need to connect this learning with the particulars of your brand. Research will still be necessary along the way, but it can be very specific and efficient for your needs. First you need to get ready by following the preliminary steps.

Step 1: Dream
Start with a dream. If you are a true marketer at heart, you will know what I am talking about.

You need to dream for your brand in terms of ultimate possibilities, for only when you have the right goal in mind can you develop a feasible strategy. Perhaps your goals are actually modest. That's okay, and sometimes practical, even smart. But imagination is free, so begin by asking how high is up:

- What if my brand became the world leader in its category among youth?
- What if young people started buying my brand now and continued buying it for a lifetime?
- What if I could line extend my product into new categories?
- What if I could increase the average frequency of repeat purchasing?
- What if I could command a higher price for my brand?
- What if I could expand into new countries or regions, capturing the market?
- What if I could sell directly to my target over the Internet?
- What if I became my target's favorite brand? What would all the relevant possibilities be?

Step 2: Reality Check
Next, do a thorough reality check. What are the essential costs and hurdles associated with achieving this dream? How should the dream be realistically modified into an achievable goal?

Step 3: Take Stock
This is a most crucial step. Assess the strengths and weaknesses of the brand.

- What is my brand's competitive advantage, if any?
- What is my brand's personality?
- What brands are my toughest competitors, and why?
- How does my brand look on the shelf?
- Is my brand competitively priced?
- How does my target learn about the brand? Is there adequate advertising, promotion, sponsorships, signage, public relations, education, sampling, and so on to let teens know my brand exists and what it stands for?
- How well does my product perform? Does it live up to its promises, or do I need to make excuses about how it works?

The key is to be honest. Take off the rose-colored glasses, because your target isn't wearing them, and answer this question honestly: Why would anyone in their right mind buy your brand over your competitors'? Being "me too" is never enough. You have to ultimately have a tiebreaker that makes the hand go to your brand.

I know this all sounds terribly simplistic, but after 25 years of working with countless product managers and advertising executives on almost every category known to humanity, I am amazed by the high numbers of marketers who cannot begin to adequately answer that question.

Step 4: Do Research

The truth is, if you can't answer this question (and there is no shame in that), you need to go directly to the target consumer. You also have to shop for the product in multiple outlets, and use the product, as well as your competitors. Don't just look at the numbers. Wear the jeans, run in the shoes, eat the candy, shave with the razor, whatever.

The surest way to understand what a brand has going for it is to talk to loyal or heavy users. These are the people who can fill a two-hour focus group singing the praises of your brand and then hang around afterward because they are so worked up by the topic.

Step 5: Get Organized

The prep work you have done so far has been to develop the tools and ammunition to develop a global strategy. Next, you need to immerse yourself in the learning. Take over a conference room and paper the walls with competitors' ads, packages, pictures of the target, photos of the product in use, and so on.

By the way, if your plans are international, your input needs to be international. For example, who's the competition in China? What does their packaging and advertising look like?

Step 6: Profile Your Prime Prospect

Develop some synopses and photos of prospective users around the world. Contrast these people with competitive users. What do they look like? How do they spend their day? What segment are they in? What does your brand mean to them now? What could it mean to them tomorrow?

Step 7: Get the Big Picture

What countries do you want to target? What are the respective populations in your target and brand positioning markets? What are the differences between markets where your brand is already strong versus where it is weak, where it is new versus where it is emerging?

Assess where your brand is already strong and where new inroads can easily be made. For instance, if your brand is Cover Girl, consider Taiwan and China. Makeup for girls is just begging to take off there, and the market could be yours to claim.

Step 8: Ladder Your Assets

It is very useful to organize your brand's attributes, benefits, and values along a ladder to help make connections in the consumer's mind.

Start with the physical attributes. If you are Coca-Cola, you are cold, wet, and amber. If you are a Mars bar, you are chocolatey, chewy, and creamy.

Sample ladder.

COCA-COLA

Values:	Renewal of spirit

↑

Emotional benefits:	Refreshment, pause to reflect

↑

Functional benefit:	Thirst-quenching, hydrating

↑

Attributes:	Cold, wet, sweet, amber

MILKY WAY/MARS BAR

Values:	Empowerment

↑

Emotional benefits:	Self-reward, comfort

↑

Functional benefits:	Hunger satisfaction, energy

↑

Attributes:	Chocolatey, chewy, caramel, sweet, rich

Next, state your brand's functional benefits. These could be thirst-quenching, hydrating, hunger-satisfying, energizing, and so on.

Then comes the rich territory of emotional benefits.

Coca-Cola offers refreshment, a pause to reflect social sharing. Mars bars offer a self-reward, or comfort. As I said when I was the strategic planner for the brand at D'Arcy—giving rise to unbridled laughter from my colleagues—"Milky Way is a hug for your mouth."

Finally, make a leap to the ultimate value you provide. Coca-Cola provides renewal of the spirit, Milky Way, or Mars bar as it is known internationally, provides empowerment.

Perhaps you do not agree. Perhaps you can think of several other cogent attributes, benefits, and values of these brands. Chances are you would also be right. In the world of marketing strategy, many roads lead to Mecca. The important thing is to choose ideas for your ladder that ring true to the brand and are potentially powerful in their appeal to your target. Try alternate ladders, and then talk them over with your consumers. Like love, you will know when it feels right.

Step 9: Evaluate Your Brand through the Lens of Global Unifiers— Create Your Own Luck

I once heard *luck* defined as "when preparation meets opportunity." If you have made the right efforts researching and analyzing your brand, you will have done the preparation to leverage the opportunity of global youth unifiers. This, in turn, will bring your brand marketing luck.

This is the stage where you need to operate both lobes of the brain—the rational left brain and the creative right brain.

Ask yourself: If my brand, like Coca-Cola, stands for renewal of the spirit, how can I link this with a marketing and communication program that links to hope or self-reliance? What can I do in the area of hope, sensation, sports, or entertainment? The opportunities are as endless as your imagination.

Step 10: Fine-Tune Your Target

Consider your product from the standpoint of benefits and brand personality. Are there some segments that would more naturally gravitate to the brand? Is the product a fashion brand that is really out there or cutting edge? If you are Calvin Klein, it is probably the thrills-and-chills trendsetters, who are a little irreverent and eager to look sophisticated, who will be your easiest mark. If you are Ralph Lauren or Tommy Hilfiger, on the other hand, it's probably the bootstrappers, who want to appear appropriately adult and preppy, who will gravitate toward your product.

Step 11: Assess the Differentiators

Ask what is there about your target that might pose a stumbling block to certain market segments or regions. If your appeal is overtly sexy, such as Calvin Klein's or the new Levi's ad where a kid is caught with his pants down, forget about most of Asia, or change your advertising tone and manner for that region.

My all-time favorite example was the international translation of the Mars Bounty coconut bar for advertising for the Middle East. In Europe and the United States, D'Arcy had developed a powerful visual commercial showing a voluptuous woman walking out of the ocean onto a beach. Dripping wet, she exuded moisture and sensory delight. Waiting for her was a handsome young man. In the Middle East—you guessed it—we could only show the man.

Step 12: Be Real and Respectful

The best way to think of global youth is as a 35-year-old head on a 15-year-old body, with a fine-tuned BS meter. If your message talks down to teens, infantilizes them, or attempts to bamboozle them, the loss will be yours.

Some of the most notable advertising to leverage this understanding is done by the American Ad Council in its antidrug campaign aimed at youth. One of its most powerful ads ever starts with a close-up of an egg. "This is your brain," the announcer says. Next you see a teenage girl smashing the egg with an iron frying pan. You hear the voiceover say, "This is your brain on drugs," as the egg splatters all over the kitchen. Direct, honest, arresting, the message comes loud and clear without sugarcoating or condescension. It is also unforgettable.

The other aspect of being real and respectful is to loop back to your target with any major communication programs or investments. If your campaign is intended to be humorous—and teens love humor—show it to your target audience. It had better make them laugh.

Perhaps you are wondering how much research is enough. One CMO I know always asked me to do research that was quick and dirty. He would then flinch, expecting to receive some verbal barb or holier-than-thou lecture about my pristine research standards. The truth is, I knew that what he meant was "Don't blow the whole budget or take as long as you would need to get a PhD." He needed a cost-effective answer.

My rule of thumb, having conducted every kind of research known to humanity throughout a 25-year career, is *what will it take to get close to the truth?* If you want to know if it's raining, you only need to stick your head out the window. You do not need a thousand measurements unless the challenge addresses several miles of terrain.

On the other hand, if you want to understand the global usage patterns of your product or what the dreams of a new generation are, somebody is going to have to pack their bags and start searching. If you need to develop demand forecasts for a new product concept, then your research methodology needs to be carefully designed and quantitative.

What makes the conclusions in this book reliable is that they are based on a huge quantitative study that was carefully sample balanced and weighted for geography, gender, and socioeconomic status. But if you only want to know if the joke is funny. . . .

The Kind of Advertising Teens Like

Conventional wisdom for general advertising says that certain elements are almost guaranteed to work. These are babies, brides, and pets. People are emotional suckers for all three. This partly explains the popularity of the recent rash of successful animal spots in the United States, with a spokesdog for Taco Bell fast food, spokesfrogs for Budweiser beer, and even a spokesparrot for Whiskas cat food. Even the new Philips CD recorder ad stacks the deck, showing not just one animal, but a dog, a bird, and a fish.

Another surefire way to succeed is to follow this age-old advisory: "If your client's flaming mad, put your client in the ad."

This has worked historically to make national celebrities of Orville Redenbacher, Frank Perdue, Victor Kiam, and Dave Thomas, to name a few. For teens it's useful to think of the target as your client. This is why Calvin Klein's "real people" campaign and the new Gap campaign showing wonderfully attractive teens wearing Gap clothes and singing "Mellow Yellow" are so powerful. There is nothing so fascinating to teens as looking at each other, especially if the teens shown are real. Teens love to size each other up. What's she wearing? Who's he with? Look at that hair! Teens have radar for statements of style, coolness, and innovation. Many want to express their individuality, but often that expression is a variation of an accepted theme. For my generation, it was my tie-dyed clothing versus your tie-dyed clothing, but it was tie-dyed all the same. Now it's my tattoo or henna design versus yours, and so on.

So let's say you're a creative director and you've just landed the Acme Nose-Ring account. Where do you start? Well, here's some important things to know.

In Wave I of the D'Arcy New World Teen Study, we surveyed 6,400 teens throughout 26 countries on the question of what kind of advertising best appeals to people their age. In a sense, this is what the generation is giving you as their advice, and they should know:

Top 10 Types of Advertising Appeals among Teens

1. Make me laugh.
2. Be fun.
3. Use popular music.
4. Be realistic.
5. Use young actors (male and female).
6. Use contemporary colors and graphics.
7. Use special effects.
8. Show the product in use.
9. Tell an interesting story.
10. Show that the company cares.

What was ranked last? "Simply show what the product is and does." This is often the desire of manufacturers who are in love with their products and assume that everyone else should be, as well.

The truth is, there is one cardinal rule of advertising that is especially true when targeting teens: "Thou shalt not be boring!"

If you examine the creative reels of the marketers profiled in this book, and other successful brand advertising aimed at teens, you will see commercials that utilize at least half of these elements, and sometimes all of them. It's common sense to stack the deck and use elements that have a high probability of working.

Nonetheless, when it comes to creativity there should never be formulas—just important principles and insights that you can put in your brain, forget where they came from, and then have reemerge as a totally new and fresh idea. This is the real magic of marketing.

Hopefully, this chapter has inspired you to think like the world's most successful marketers and go through the analytic discipline as well as the creative leapfrogs necessary to achieve new heights for your brand.

9

The Fabric
of Everyday Life

Teens the world over lead parallel lives. Up early, off to school.
Seven hours of intensive classes and study. After school, sports
and activities. Then home to snacks, music, television, computers,
talking on the phone, helping Mom, and doing homework. The
modern rituals of being a teenager are remarkably uniform
throughout the world due to the globalization of culture.

My vision of a typical teen is someone who is multitasking—
doing homework, talking on the phone, chatting online, listening to music or watching television, eating something—all at the
same time. Just think, it is possible that your advertising exposure, be it through radio, print, television, or Web site, may be
competing for a teen's attention with three other ads, all at the
same time.

In order to understand the new world teen generation, you
need to know their natural habits and habitats. You need to have

a feel for the fabric of everyday life. How do teens spend their time? What do they do for enjoyment? What kinds of movies and television shows do they watch? Do they like to watch sports or just play them? This chapter examines the rituals and behaviors of teen culture in contrast with the internal values and drivers discussed previously. It focuses on typical patterns of behavior and their implications for marketers.

The Architecture of Time

Beyond sleep and school attendance, a teen's life is dominated by socializing with friends and family, watching television, pursuing leisure interests, and listening to the radio. Homework and chores receive relatively less attention. Based on findings from the Philips Navigator Study on global consumer lifestyle and technology in 17 countries, it is clear that the structure of a teen's day is different from that of all other age groups in two main areas. Sleep is the first area. Teens sleep an average of 7.9 hours a night, which is at least a half-hour more than adults. Socializing is the second area of difference. Teens spend an hour more socializing than adults. Perhaps most surprising is the fact that teens spend approximately the same amount of time as adults watching television and listening to the radio. This is most likely because they are equally pressured for time and are pulled in many directions. The passivity required for watching television and listening to the radio is a luxury often threatened by escalating responsibilities.

While the levels stated here reflect the amount of time spent on a typical day in a teenager's life, they do not tell the whole story. This is because there are several other factors that befall a teen's life that can impact how a typical day, and especially a weekend, is likely to go.

Activity Time Teens and Adults Spent in One Day, in Hours

Activity	Teens (Age 15–18)		Adults (Age 19–65)
Sleep	7.9	←	7.2
Socializing	3.3	←	2.3
Watching television	2.4		2.3
Listening to radio	1.3		1.2
Pursuing leisure interests	1.7	←	1.1
Doing homework or chores	0.9	→	1.5
Exercising/playing sports	0.7		0.3
Taking care of pets	0.7		0.6
Talking on phone	0.4		0.4

The bottom line is that teens the world over (90 percent) are expected to get good grades. This is job one. So if only an hour is being spent on homework on average, the weight of responsibility must still rest heavily on the mind. Beyond grade management, half of all teens are expected to help clean the house; 1 in 3 are required to take care of brothers and sisters; 1 in 4 are required to prepare meals; and 1 in 5 must do laundry. Almost 1 in 3 are also expected to work outside the home for money. This adds up to a full spectrum of adult responsibilities on top of the school requirements that are essential to teen life. Perhaps so many teens seem mature nowadays because they have little time for the classic shenanigans of idle youth.

It should also be noted that expectations for teens are generally the same for both genders, with a couple of almost clichéd exceptions. Girls have higher levels of responsibility for traditional housework—cleaning, cooking, and laundering. Boys are required to take care of the lawn or garden and earn more money than girls.

Perhaps somewhat surprising is that only 15 percent of teens worldwide are expected to shop for groceries. This means that they are not likely to be choosing the brands of fabric softener or

Global Teen Responsibilities

	Percentage		
Responsibility	Total	Males	Females
Get good grades	90	91	90
Clean the house	51	43	60
Care for brothers/sisters	37	36	37
Work/earn money	31	35	28
Take care of pets	29	28	31
Prepare meals	23	17	30
Do laundry	22	17	28
Take care of elderly relatives	19	19	18
Take care of lawn/garden	16	24	8
Shop for groceries	15	14	16

canned peas. This is not to imply, however, that teens do not have a strong influence over food brand choice, or do not purchase certain items on their own, because they do so significantly. It means that the family grocery shopping is one of the few adult household management responsibilities that does not sit firmly on their shoulders.

Food Habits

Conventional wisdom tells us that teens have voracious appetites. This is a life-stage phenomenon, because at adolescence there are tremendous growth and energy expenditures, and food requirements increase to support these patterns. What teens get at home for dinner is very much a function of the local road of the dual cultural passport. However, what they eat on their own tends to be from the global fast food lane.

At the top of the list for past-week consumption is candy and confectionery, with an almost ubiquitous (82 percent) incidence. Clearly, teens the world over have an exceptional sweet tooth,

Foods Global Teens Consumed in Past Week

Food	Percentage	Food	Percentage
Candy/confectionery	82	Tea/iced tea	58
Juice	76	Fresh salad	52
Fresh vegetables	75	Ice cream/frozen yogurt	51
Chewing gum	71	Fast food	51
Soda/carbonated beverages	69	Coffee	49
Salty snacks	66	Hamburger	40
Cakes/cookies	64	Pizza	36

with considerable indulgence in chewing gum, chocolate bars, baked goods, ice cream, and carbonated sodas. However, salty snacks are also consumed at least weekly by 2 out of 3 teens worldwide.

Perhaps more surprising are the facts that Junior is eating his vegetables, with a 75 percent incidence, and that our young adults are drinking coffee and tea. Fast food in general is consumed by half of teens worldwide on a weekly or more frequent basis—about the same level as fresh green salads. Only 12 percent of teens worldwide claim to be vegetarian, although levels vary by regions and religious beliefs.

It should also be noted that more than 1 in 3 teens worldwide are expected to pay for their own snacks and beverages.

Personal Care

Today's teen is clean! Almost all teens brush their teeth and take a bath or a shower daily. This clearly was not always the case globally, but modern plumbing and standards have overcome historical habits. Moreover, it should be kept in mind that at the teenage life stage, attention to appearance is crucially important, particularly for those who are looking to attract romantic interest. Nonetheless,

Global Teens' Daily Grooming

Activity	Percentage
Brush teeth	95
Wash face with soap/cleanser	77
Shower	70
Wash hair	58
Use mouthwash	39
Use hair conditioner	36
Use acne medication	24
Bathe in tub	22
Use dental floss	22
Use bath additive	15

waves of teenage styles from hippiedom to grunge have created episodes of culture when dirty clothes and stringy hair prevailed. But that is now, as we say, history. Today's teen is clean and projects positive self-maintenance.

On the other hand, from a marketer's perspective, use of personal care products is neither universal nor consistent from country to country. Only 1 in 3 teens uses hair conditioner, 1 in 4 uses acne medication, and only 1 in 5 uses dental floss.

Fashion and Why They Dress That Way

Teenagers throughout the world realize that appearance is empowering. As they strive to become individuals and take charge of their own futures, they do a great deal of experimentation to assess effects. Anywhere in the world, a teen can suddenly one day sport a Mohawk haircut with Day-Glo green or orange highlights, a pierced tongue, and a tattoo of a snake. This kid seeks attention and respect for displaying bold individuality. This kid may also be testing relationships with parents and other authority figures, as well as making a statement of intent to be original. But truthfully, beyond all these classic psychological interpretations of youthful flamboyance is the simple, sometimes overlooked motivator of *celebration*. Most teens feel exuberant about life. Despite all their doubts and insecurities there is a sense of joy and free expression that is patterned through history in outrageous garb. Some adults tend to look at aberrant dress styles as a modern form of war paint, reflecting youthful intent toward rebellion. But those adults need to reconsider their hasty conclusions. The clothes and fashions of youth may be little more than passionate affirmation of the joy of living.

That same kid who looks like a maniac to some adults may be very worried about parents who smoke, have high ambitions for achievement, and be a staunch advocate for animal rights. In other words, caring, human, and without a single hostile bone.

Passion: Teens and Technology

I've mentioned teens and their fascination with technology in other sections of this book, but it will be helpful to devote more focus to this here because technology is essential to contemporary youth lifestyles. Why? Because technology is the most direct and efficient path to communicate with teens. It's also the path that many will take in their future careers.

In the next 10 years, advances in existing telephone and television technology will expand the speed and the format of communications exponentially. Computers, too, will be vastly different in what they can access and deliver. Connections between different technological components, like software and hardware linkages, will dramatically alter how people experience the worlds of work and leisure.

Technology is as easy for teens to understand and embrace as it is for me to walk onto an escalator. And for many members of the older generation, technology seems as frightening a prospect as an escalator seems to a remote Indian tribe.

It is important to remember that the global teen's entry into the world of technology originated in a pleasure mode. The first time was a form of entertainment, of fun—playing games and solving puzzles in a multimedia sound and picture play station or computer environment. Even in their late teens, kids of this generation worldwide continue to be drawn to computers for their game applications.

So, it's easy to understand how a skill set could easily be established if the first impression of a computer was fun and stimulating. I believe that teens feel a different emotional attachment to the computer. They respond favorably to the pleasures of technology. But don't forget, teens derive another benefit from computer use: They can empower themselves and increase their self-esteem. Using the computer is like winning the jackpot on a slot machine: It pays off in successful operation when it's used correctly. And teens know how to use computers, so they receive daily reinforcement that they have succeeded. Teens around the world will be in the forefront of all technological advances.

The Truer Picture: Statistical Data

Here are many different statistics that describe a precise portrait of how teens perceive technology. For contrast, I have included data from other age groups so that you can see the differences and the similarities between generations.

Some of the data come from the Philips Navigator Survey completed in 1999 in 17 countries with 14,000 respondents, of whom 2,300 were teenagers.

Computer Users Who Use the Computer for Games

Region	Percentage	Region	Percentage
Africa	82	Asia Pacific	72
Middle East	79	India	71
Eastern Europe	76	United States	70
Western Europe	75	China	62
Latin America	72		

Computer Access

Not surprisingly, teens ages 13 to 18 rank as the highest among all age groups in computer usage. More than 50 percent of this segment has had access to a computer in the past 30 days (54 percent). Contrast this tally with only 30 percent of the 60-plus group, and you can see the significant difference between young and old. The data for access to a computer in the past 30 days follow.

Past 30 Day Computer Access

Age	Percentage
13 to 18	54
19 to 29	49
30 to 39	41
40 to 59	39
60+	30

I predict that over the next 10 years these percentages will increase across the board for all age segments. The prices of computers are dropping significantly, new computers will be even more user-friendly, and, significantly, many more practical uses, including shopping, will be linked to computers.

Web Usage

The unanswered question today is how fast the United States and the rest of the world will begin to access the Internet. Currently, Philips's research reveals that Web usage for the entire survey population is 7 percent, with teens' usage at 8 percent.

These numbers will rise substantially over the next 10 years, and all indexes point to the fact that teens' Internet usage will increase at a dramatically higher rate than that of the general population. An important fact to know, if you're marketing to teens.

Teens' Computer Usage

Global teens use computers for many reasons, but game playing ranks the highest. This comes as no surprise given teens' constant need for sensation and love of fun. Note in the following data on how teens use computers that games applications supersede schoolwork.

Teen's Computer Applications

Activity	Percentage
Games	30
School work	22
Word processing	21
Learning	21

School Is the Answer

Most teens in developing countries who have access to computers have their schools to thank. Countries such as Peru, Mexico, and Colombia have wisely realized that providing computer access will be the fastest way for the next generation to catch up with the global economy.

The table shows the top 10 out of 44 teen study countries where computers are accessed at school in major markets. Note that all inhabited continents are represented, but that the United States, at 72 percent, just misses the top-10 list. This is because teens in America more often use computers at home.

Top 10 Countries: Computer Users Who Use Computers at School

1. Peru	90%
2. Denmark	84
3. Hong Kong	81
4. Mexico	81
5. Australia	78
6. United Kingdom	78
7. Belgium	76
8. Colombia	75
9. Israel	74
10. Argentina	74

Attitudes toward Technology

Teens view the advent of new technology with the same expectant enthusiasm with which they regard the arrival of a favorite band's new CD. Something cool and fun is coming their way, and they can hardly wait: 35 percent state that they are highly enthusiastic about technology. Some 32 percent like to get involved in new technology. Interestingly, they also have a practical sense: 46 percent state that new technology must be mastered if a person is to remain up to date.

Only 10 percent of teens state that technology is beyond them. This figure compares to 34 percent of the general population who believe technology is beyond them—more than three times the total for teens. In other words, there is virtually no resistance among this young cohort.

If you are selling your product via e-commerce, teens are actively looking for goods to buy. The question yet to be fully answered is whether the Internet will turn into a brand emporium, a bargain basement, an artisan boutique, or all three. The data for who would like to shop by computer follow.

Would Like to Shop by Computer

Age	Percentage
13 to 18	54
19 to 29	43
30 to 39	46
40 to 59	49
60+	36

Computer Time versus Television Time

Teens in the Philips study spent 1.4 hours per day at home on the computer. This is actually less than the average of 1.5 hours per day for adults. But the finding is not surprising. Teens are very busy every day with schoolwork, sports and exercise, school clubs, work (in the United States), socializing with friends, and helping out at home.

A more significant statistic is computer usage outside the home. Adults spend about 2.5 hours per day (mostly work related) using computers, while it's less for teens, at 1.6 hours per day.

Teens spend 2.7 hours per day watching television, which is slightly higher than the 2.6 hours per day for adults. Remember, though, that when teens are watching the tube, they are also multitasking: studying, participating in chat rooms on the Internet, or talking to friends on the telephone.

The Six Teen Value Segments and Technology

Marketers must recognize that there are differences in access to technology among the six different teen value segments first outlined in Chapter 5. Thrills-and-chills teens lead the pack in having computers at home. This is no surprise, because these kids come from parents who are more affluent. Data for having a computer at home (average is 23 percent) follow.

Home Access to a Computer

Segment	Percentage
Thrills and chills	31
Bootstrappers	25
Resigned	24
World savers	24
Quiet achievers	17
Upholders	15

18 percent of the thrills-and-chills teens are online, compared with 13 percent globally. These kids are high-touch and high-involvement computer users. They are pushing the envelope on e-commerce and are actively looking for more—and more interesting—places to shop. Data for online access follow.

Global Online Access

Segment	Percentage
Thrills and chills	18
Resigned	15
Bootstrappers	14
World savers	14
Quiet achievers	11
Upholders	9

Technological Attitudinal Responses

In the last part of the Philips Navigator Survey we asked both teens and adults questions about technology expectations. What I found interesting is that for all their computer knowledge, teens realize that they don't have all the answers when it comes to the future of technology.

For example, only 20 percent of teens agreed with the statement, "I consider myself to be very knowledgeable about new technology products," as compared with only 14 percent of the general population. It seems to me that teens are humble in evaluating their own knowledge about this industry. The data for who wants to learn to use advanced technology follow.

Desire to Learn Advanced Technology

Age	Percentage
13 to 18	66
19 to 29	64
30 to 39	56
40 to 59	59
60+	35

Teens are almost twice as eager to learn about technological advances as the oldest segment of adults. The average for this question was 53 percent. This is why adults often look to teens as being experts on advanced technology, from computers to MP3 players.

Attitudinally, protechnology sentiment is significantly higher for the 13- to 18-year-old group than for any of the other age segments at majority levels.

- 71 percent of teens agreed with the statement, "Technology makes me feel involved and connected."
- 69 percent of teens agreed with the statement, "The more I understand technology, the more I find ways to use it."
- 64 percent of teens agreed with the statement, "New technology allows me to do things I couldn't do in the past."

Let Me Entertain You

A core universal driver of teens is their obsession with fun, in infinite varieties. Teens have so many outlets for enjoyment that it's a wonder how they get any schoolwork done.

At the top of the list is music—even edging out spending time with friends, because it can be done alone. As my own teen, Zack, said to me recently, "Music is my life." Watching television, of course, is a passion at almost twice the level of playing with computers or video games.

Teens also love going to movies, watching movies on television, and playing videotapes or DVDs. While taste runs the gamut, youth's love of comedy and adventure is almost universal. What sells movie tickets can also make for effective advertising and brand positioning. To make teens laugh, with all the pressure and uncertainty they face, or to give them an escapist thrill is a reward in and of itself. And perhaps more surprising are some of the lesser activities that still represent huge numbers of teens.

Worldwide Teen Enjoyment Activities

Top 10 Activities	
Activity	Percentage
1. Listening to tapes/CDs	81
2. Watching television	79
3. Spending time with friends	77
4. Playing sports	53
5. Going shopping	44
6. Watching sports	41
7. Listening to the radio	59
8. Watching a movie at home	56
9. Going to a movie	53
10. Reading books/talking on the phone (tie)	51
Other Acceptable Activities	
Activity	Percentage
Spending time with family	36
Playing games/cards	36
Bike-riding	35
Reading comic books	30
Taking care of pets	29
Taking photos	28
Camping/hiking	26
Working on hobby	24
Cooking/baking	24

A Moving Target

What is striking to me as a social observer is the uniformity of the generation's daily life on a global basis. With common interests, common concerns, and common access to the global marketplace of experience, there is more uniformity among today's teenagers than among any other age group in the spectrum—or in history, for that matter.

However, this steady drumbeat does not last. When teens graduate to become twentysomethings, lifestyles splinter into a prism of alternatives. Consider that you can be 25 with no known address, crashing at one friend's house after another—or, you can be married with two kids and a mortgage, working at a dot-com. In some ways, life gets easier as we age because the blanks get filled in. But the wheels get set in motion and we all go our own ways. In other words, once youth hits the job market, it loses its ease of access as a huge, homogeneous, target group for marketers.

10

Beyond 2000

With global culture changing at digital speed, one has to wonder how transient these findings about global youth culture might be.

It helps to have some perspective on what is a *trend* versus what is a *fad*. If one sets out to do an international survey on teenagers' favorite pop stars around the globe, the information may be out of date by the time it is tabulated. Teens' tastes in music, movies, and fashion are easily swayed by whatever new entities pop up on the scene. These surface attitudes and behaviors count as fads.

If, on the other hand, you wish to understand the internal values and drivers of the generation, these elements are part of the fabric of the enduring psyche. Values never change abruptly; they only evolve. This means that as marketers we can examine the values of new world teens now and be confident that they will remain relatively intact throughout the generation's lifetime. They are long-term trends. What will change is how they are manifest. The key values, unifiers, and differentiators observed in this book all qualify as trends.

Subject to significant change, these will be the values of the teen generations that follow. This is because value formation is so influenced by what is happening during teens' coming of age and the personal as well as generational worldview that follows.

Stated simply, the members of the new world teen generation that we describe in this book will continue to be self-reliant, innovation-loving humanists who will try to create their own good lives using all the means of political freedom, economic opportunity, and advanced technology available. While this is likely to be the same for their younger brothers and sisters who will enter high school in 2010, only time will tell. But we can predict the implications of current trends with some confidence, assuming they have every good reason to continue.

Some Closing Advice to Marketers

Keep an eye on the trends. This advice extends to population data and economic indicators, as well as the cultural behavior of the current youth generation.

It is also critical not to lose sight of what your brand stands for to each new generation and how your brand's values link with the values of the next generation.

All global leadership brands are subject to public opinion. Consider the momentum that built, for instance, in France in the fall of 1999, when anti-U.S. backlash caused farmers to target McDonald's as an American symbol. Hopefully, McDonald's continues to monitor its image with French youth, Western European youth, and, for that matter, global youth, because these seeds of disparagement threaten to harm a positive global icon.

Just as The Coca-Cola Company reviews major world news and asks, what this means for Coca-Cola, so all global teen marketers need to keep abreast of the fast-paced marketplace and ask themselves, "What opportunities can this event possibly provide for my brand?"

Perhaps the notion of monitoring global trends seems daunting. However, there are a number of ways to achieve this insight without spending millions of dollars or reinventing the wheel:

- Syndicated trends studies
- Trend gurus
- Internet market watch
- Periodic custom research

Each approach can help marketers keep current with the changing marketplace to avoid being blindsided by threats and stay open to new brand-building opportunities.

Syndicated Trends Studies

Syndicated trends studies keep a continuing eye on the youth market in multiple countries. The New World Teen Study is a prime example of this type of research; other resources include the Roper Reports Worldwide, from Roper Starch; or Technographics, a lifestyle and attitudes study focusing on technology, from Forrester Research.

Trend Gurus

My fellow trend gurus tend to be provocative, insightful, culture watchers who reflect on the world at large and understand trend implications for marketers. The good ones rely on a combination of facts and instinct. This is what makes them special. My own list of good ones includes Marian Salzman, director of the Brand Futures Group; Watts Wacker, founder of FirstMatter; Faith Popcorn, CEO of BrainReserve; and Chris Gentle, of the Henley Centre. Sometimes marketers need an intense infusion of candid reality. All of these trends virtuosos can be relied upon to deliver that, and then some, in the context of relevance to your brand.

Internet Market Watch

Select bright up-and-comers in your organization and have them start monitoring the Internet for salient news about your target and category. One of the amazing by-products of this new age is free information. To some degree, value has shifted from the information itself to knowing how to analyze it and apply new learning. However, the least an organization can do is be sure not to miss the critical insight that is given away free. Have your own market watcher prepare an e-mail newsletter and make it widely available. Another axiom for the new millennium is that information will be more powerful when it is shared instead of guarded. (What a change!)

Periodic Custom Research

Sometimes marketers have to conduct their own proprietary research when there are no other sources and the desired information is critical to the future of a brand. This can range from qualitative research on how your advertising communicates to large-scale market studies that investigate key strategic variables on usage habits and attitudes toward your brand. The not-so-hidden warning here is that marketers must not become overly confident in guessing. Once in a while your seasoned instincts can be sufficient in light of limited time or funds. However, too much guessing about critical issues usually catches up with marketers—for the worst.

So What?

I began this book by explaining that many youth marketers are missing the boat in their understanding of today's global teen market. This insight led to extensive global research and a worldview of teenagers that provides practical direction for marketers.

If youth is your target, there are efficient ways to reach them across a wide span of geography. But first, you must throw away your assumptions, build on what is shared in this book, and then go out and *meet your target.* Spend time with teens at local community centers such as CityKids in New York, or observe them in their natural habitats, such as shopping malls, concerts, movie theaters, and fast-food restaurants.

It helps to have this foundation of understanding, but you still need to get to know and observe your target teens, particularly in the context of your brand and how it fits into their lives. Only then will your marketing efforts become vastly more effective. New ideas will flow easily and today's global teen market, the first of the millennium, will readily embrace your brand. Good luck!

Appendix

A Word about the Research

The foundation for *The $100 Billion Allowance* is based on two massive global quantitative studies—the New World Teen Study and the Philips Navigator Segmentation Study. Some detail on the methodology of each follows.

The New World Teen Study

The New World Teen Study is the largest and most comprehensive study of teen lifestyle, attitudes, and behavior ever conducted. It was sponsored by D'Arcy Masius Benton & Bowles and later managed by the BrainWaves Group.

The study was conducted in two waves. Wave I covered 26 countries with 6,400 interviews, and Wave II was conducted in 44 countries and 27,600 interviews. All participants were high school students ages 15 to 19. Sampling was done in high schools in urban and suburban markets. Questionnaires were self-completed in each country's language and returned anonymously. A donation was made to Unicef on behalf of each participating school.

A total of approximately 400 teens was sampled in each market, divided by gender. Augmented samples of 1,000 or more were established in the United States, Indonesia, Germany, Mexico, Brazil, India, and China. Questionnaires were centrally tabulated by Essex Tabulating. The values segmentation was created by myself and Chip Walker, with Dr. Ken Warwick of Warwick & Associates. Professor Shalom Schwartz of Tel Aviv University served as a consultant on cross-cultural values.

All *global totals* that are referenced from this study reflect the weighted universe of the New World Teen Study that is based on the urban and suburban teen population ages 15 to 19 in each of the 44 countries that is considered *broad middle class* by Standard & Poor's Data Resources, Inc. (DRI) data. DRI furnished the weights for urban, suburban, and broad-middle-class definitions.

Table A.1 details the weekly estimated spending by teens in each country, along with the population figures used to derive annual total teen spending for the universe of countries, where all data were available. Table A.2 details the incidence of each values segment by country. The countries included in Table A.2, listed by region, are as follows:

Africa	**Eastern Europe**	**Middle East**
Nigeria	*(Continued)*	Israel
South Africa	Lithuania	**Latin America**
China	Poland	Argentina
Eastern Europe	Russia	Brazil
Estonia	Ukraine	Chile
Hungary	**India**	Colombia
Latvia		Mexico

Latin America	Western Europe	Asia Pacific
(Continued)	(Continued)	(Continued)
Peru	Italy	Japan
Venezuela	Netherlands	Philippines
Western Europe	Norway	Singapore
Belgium	Spain	South Korea
Denmark	Sweden	Taiwan
England	Turkey	Thailand
Finland	**Asia Pacific**	Vietnam
France	Australia	**North America**
Germany	Hong Kong	Canada
Greece	Indonesia	United States

The Philips Navigator Segmentation Study

The Philips Navigator Segmentation Study was conducted to explore the values, attitudes and category behavior of the global consumer with respect to electronics and technology. A total of 14,000 personal interviews were conducted by Roper Starch Worldwide across major metro markets in 17 countries. The ages of participants spanned a range of 13 to 65, of both genders. For purpose of this analysis we focused on the global sample of 2,253 teens ages 15 to 19. The following countries were included in this study:

Argentina	Hong Kong	Poland
Brazil	India	Russia
Chile	Indonesia	Sweden
China	Italy	United Kingdom
France	Japan	United States
Germany	Mexico	

Table A.1   Annual Estimated Teen Spending Adjusted by Broad Middle Class and Urban/ Suburban Residence[1]

Country, by Region	Weekly Spending per Teen[2]	Teen Population Ages 15–19[3]	Adjusted Annual Estimated Teen Spending
Africa			
Nigeria[4]	$ 6.50	12,074,225	$ 163,243,522.00
South Africa[5]	18.80	4,529,189	1,562,104,966.71
Asia/Pacific			
Australia[5]	25.30	1,271,988	1,351,292,635.84
China[5]	5.50	97,698,459	3,739,725,061.23
Hong Kong	38.00	446,658	751,265,892.25
India[5]	27.50	101,310,415	16,460,571,773.79
Indonesia[5]	8.60	22,324,861	818,661,582.81
Japan	24.40	7,675,243	7,048,616,512.86
Philippines[5]	14.50	8,408,864	1,710,608,476.43
Singapore	34.10	207,002	357,879,547.74
South Korea	19.70	3,849,969	2,713,408,871.60
Taiwan[5]	22.40	1,951,457	1,551,361,480.03
Thailand[6]	20.30	5,709,091	4,230,614,554.64
Vietnam[5]	4.40	8,467,502	227,175,356.30
Eastern Europe			
Hungary	5.60	674,523	110,310,088.41
Lithuania[5]	8.60	264,790	69,059,096.12
Poland	10.60	3,354,481	1,053,184,662.53
Russia[5]	7.40	11,672,788	3,004,041,484.42
Latin America			
Argentina[5]	40.50	3,265,876	5,066,011,697.54
Brazil[5]	41.30	17,785,949	14,705,885,067.87
Chile[4]	5.60	1,321,713	129,320,629.40
Colombia[5]	21.50	3,631,455	1,718,989,896.55
Mexico[5]	12.80	10,701,137	2,528,550,259.46
Peru[5]	18.40	2,754,550	781,125,328.55
Venezuela[4,6]	12.40	2,370,272	573,131,769.60
North America			
Canada[5]	19.60	2,065,261	1,555,952,437.08
United States[5]	37.60	19,675,722	26,959,756,135.40

Table A.1   (Continued)

Country, by Region	Weekly Spending per Teen[2]	Teen Population Ages 15–19[3]	Adjusted Annual Estimated Teen Spending
Western Europe			
Belgium[5]	21.20	614,863	558,866,688.75
Denmark[4]	37.40	286,022	461,692,136.05
France[5]	31.30	3,921,055	2,606,882,236.52
Germany	29.6	4,548,827	5,720,270,041.53
Greece[5]	32.90	740,963	758,682,240.99
Netherlands	23.10	918,361	952,336,646.82
Norway[4]	49.70	264,320	478,176,025.60
Spain[5]	15.60	2,656,907	1,510,206,768.95
Sweden	41.70	505,514	870,129,075.42
United Kingdom[5]	26.30	3,697,470	4,466,042,087.27
Totals	$863.80	373,617,742	$119,325,132,735.06

[1]Based on Standard & Poor's Data Resources, Inc. (DRI) data.

[2]New World Teen Study, Wave II.

[3]U.S. Bureau of the Census, International Data Base, 1999.

[4]Percentage of middle class was estimated based on figures for similar countries.

[5]Percentage of middle class was estimated for the entire country based on the urban/suburban middle class figure.

[6]Percentage of urban/suburban population estimated from the figures for similar countries.

Table A.2   New World Teen Study Segment Incidence by Country

Country, by Region	Segment					
	Thrills and Chills	Resigned	Bootstrappers	World Savers	Upholders	Quiet Achievers
Africa						
Nigeria	3%	10%	41%	13%	16%	2%
South Africa	32	12	16	15	11	5
Asia/Pacific						
Australia	22	14	17	16	8	5
China	5	3	8	4	29	44
Hong Kong	12	11	12	11	17	21
India	8	15	23	12	19	10
Indonesia	4	4	4	7	64	9
Japan	24	38	4	4	7	9
Philippines	9	8	16	28	18	5
Singapore	16	13	11	18	18	13
South Korea	19	40	6	2	6	19
Taiwan	13	17	10	3	31	6
Thailand	5	0	1	2	2	69
Vietnam	2	3	9	5	64	12
Eastern Europe						
Estonia	21	17	10	10	20	11
Hungary	16	14	8	22	19	9
Latvia	21	15	25	1	10	17
Lithuania	34	8	16	3	11	18
Poland	24	14	14	16	17	7
Russia	16	12	10	20	14	18
Ukraine	18	12	13	15	12	20
Latin America						
Argentina	17	21	10	22	13	8
Brazil	17	8	15	24	10	12
Chile	16	12	19	15	15	8
Colombia	13	8	17	23	13	7
Mexico	9	7	35	15	16	9
Peru	11	6	18	11	24	17
Venezuela	6	11	25	23	19	6

Table A.2   (Continued)

Country, by Region	Segment					
	Thrills and Chills	Resigned	Bootstrappers	World Savers	Upholders	Quiet Achievers
Middle East						
Israel	27	15	18	3	6	12
North America						
Canada	28	21	13	12	8	6
United States	28	9	26	9	7	10
Western Europe						
Belgium	29	27	5	21	5	4
Denmark	21	46	8	6	8	2
Finland	19	39	4	6	17	6
France	24	18	4	17	7	9
Germany	37	27	9	11	5	4
Greece	32	13	14	6	15	7
Italy	23	7	10	15	27	8
Netherlands	32	26	10	10	6	7
Norway	20	38	7	13	11	4
Spain	18	21	9	24	12	7
Sweden	19	45	5	8	4	3
Turkey	27	21	10	12	8	5
United Kingdom	34	21	9	14	7	8
Global Average*	17%	14%	14%	12%	16%	15%

*12 percent of the sample is unclassified; hence, rows do not add to 100 percent.

Index

About the Author

Elissa Moses is senior vice president, director of global consumer and market intelligence for Royal Philips Electronics N.V. Leading the competency across divisions, she also serves as an internal expert on brand strategy, new product marketing, international lifestyle trends, and consumer behavior.

Prior to her position at Philips, she was founder and managing director of The BrainWaves Group, an independent global consulting, research and trends company. At BrainWaves, she created the New World Teen Study, the most extensive research ever conducted on the lifestyles and values of global youth, spanning 44 countries. Her clients included The Coca-Cola Company, Levi's, Calvin Klein, MTV, the National Basketball Association, General Motors, M&M Mars, and Kodak. Earlier, she was the director of strategic planning at DMB&B and held senior positions at BBDO, Joseph E. Seagram & Sons, and the Gillette Company.

Ms. Moses received a BA in human behavior at the University of Chicago and studied marketing at the Northwestern Graduate School of Management. Throughout her career, she has applied the psychology of human motivation to consumer marketing.

Ms. Moses has served as president of the Communications Research Council, and as chairwoman of the AMA Educational Institute. She is a founder of the AMA Career Advisory Board and serves on the board of directors for the CityKids Foundation. She is also a recipient of the 1994 YWCA Woman Achievers Award.

Ms. Moses is a frequently sought speaker throughout the world. Her forecasts and commentary have been featured in a wide array of national and international media, including the *International Herald Tribune*, the *New York Times*, *USA Today*, the *Wall Street Journal*, the *Today Show*, and NBC *Nightly News*.

Ms. Moses and her husband Mark Shornick, chief financial officer of NumeriX, reside in Westport, Connecticut, with their two teenage children, Emily and Zachary.

Elissa Moses can be reached at elissamoses@aol.com.